HARVEY HOUSES
—— of **KANSAS** ——

HARVEY HOUSES
of **KANSAS**

Historic Hospitality from Topeka to Syracuse

ROSA WALSTON LATIMER

THE
History
PRESS

Published by The History Press
Charleston, SC 29403
www.historypress.net

First published 2015

Manufactured in the United States

ISBN 978.1.62619.847.0

Library of Congress Control Number: 2015946486

CONTENTS

CONTENTS

"HARVEY GIRL"

An excerpt from the poem by Jessica Helen Lopez, Poet Laureate of Albuquerque, New Mexico, 2015

Harvey Girl we salute you
transcontinental dreams come true
going out on the line and casting your hopes
your union station stories

You woman
who fed the boys
who paved our way
who opened doors

You blue collar woman
break back break nail
wear a smile woman
You westward dream woman

You
Harvey
Girl

ACKNOWLEDGEMENTS

Thank-you to the following individuals for their help in obtaining information and images: Louise Reynolds and family; Julia Ortolon; Julie Grubbs McCombs, Kearny County Historical Society, Lakin, Kansas; Nancy Sherbert, Kansas Historical Society; and Judy Mills, Florence Historical Society. Also my appreciation to the Hamilton County Historical Society; Jane Jones and Kristine Schmucker, Harvey County Historical Society; and Connie Pennick, Depot Theater Company.

A special thank you to Carolyn Rosser, who shared photos of her Harvey Girl grandmother, Dott Rahlin. I met Carolyn at a book signing for *Harvey Houses of Texas* when I was just beginning Kansas research. I commend her for her resolve to provide images for this book, and although we were unable to determine the exact location(s) in Kansas where Dott worked as a Harvey Girl, I am pleased that we could preserve this little bit of her story.

After long searching for certain details about the Fort Scott, Kansas Harvey House, two days before the deadline for this manuscript I was directed to Arnold Schofield, a Fort Scott historian who graciously verified the information I needed. At the end of this long project, this act of kindness from a stranger was very much appreciated.

Without the help and support of Michael McMillan and his fabulous vintage postcard collection I could not have properly told this story. How fortunate I am to have become acquainted with this very talented, knowledgeable individual. Thank you, Michael, for your continued contribution to the telling of the Harvey House story!

I'm especially grateful to Danyelle Gentry Petersen and Beau Gentry for sharing the story of their father, Skip. By all accounts, Skip was a great friend to all who knew him, and his collection of Fred Harvey/Harvey House memorabilia is unsurpassed. We are fortunate to have some of Beau's photos of pieces from Skip's collection included in this book.

Thank you to the poet laureate of Albuquerque, New Mexico, Jessica Helen Lopez, for allowing me to print a portion of her poem "Harvey Girl" as an introduction to this book. I wish I could somehow embed a recording of Jessica performing the poem in its entirety. I guarantee goosebumps!

A special "shout out" to Jim and Kathy Weir. I count their friendship as one of the valuable, unexpected benefits of writing this book. I'm looking forward to more Fred Harvey/Mary Colter adventures with these two special people.

Many, many thanks to Janice Plummer for looking after all my critters, to Kathy Beach for being a wonderful traveling companion and to Melissa Morrow for her encouragement and wisdom during this project.

To my daughter and best friend, Lara: I love you and am so thankful to have you in my life. Thank you for all you do to make everything better for me.

In everything I do since meeting "His Happiness," I acknowledge his unfailing love that continues to be a profound presence in my life.

INTRODUCTION

Although this is my third book about Fred Harvey and the Harvey Girls, it is actually the beginning of the story. Kansas is where it all began—the first depot restaurant and the first combination hotel and restaurant—before the waitresses were called Harvey Girls. Mr. Harvey chose Kansas for his family's home and built a lovely house in Leavenworth. Perhaps lacking some of the flair that lured tourists to the Southwest Harvey Houses, luxurious Harvey hotels were built at strategic points along the Santa Fe Railroad as it raced across Kansas, and the Fred Harvey Company established operating headquarters for more than half of the Harvey eating system in Newton.

I first became interested in Harvey Girls when my uncle Bill provided me with a detailed family tree and pointed out that my grandmother had worn the now iconic black-and-white Harvey Girl uniform in the early 1900s. At the time I heard this family story, I had no idea what a Harvey Girl was, but I felt that if I learned about these adventuresome, hardworking women, I would also learn about my grandmother, a woman I last saw when I was two years old.

Gertrude Elizabeth McCormick met my grandfather William Alexander Balmanno in 1913 while she was working as a Harvey Girl in Rincon, New Mexico. When William was twelve years old, he left his family on the island of Mauritius in the Indian Ocean to work on whaling ships. At the age of twenty-nine, he and a friend quit their whaling jobs in Vera Cruz, Mexico, and decided to walk to California. On the way, in Rincon, William took a job with the Santa Fe Railroad to earn money to finish his trip.

My grandmother, an orphan who finished nursing school in Philadelphia, wanted to go to Alaska. (Looking for adventure, I suppose.) She reasoned that working as a Harvey Girl would be a good start as it afforded the opportunity to transfer to different locations—all the way to California. Her first assignment was at the lunch counter in the Harvey House in Rincon, where she met William. They were married three months later and spent the rest of their lives in New Mexico.

With this true story, I began my research about Harvey Girls, the Harvey Houses where they worked and Fred Harvey, the man who advertised for "educated women of good character" to come West to work. Initially, of course, my interest was in my grandparents and New Mexico Harvey Houses, but I soon became interested in the Harvey Houses of Texas. During this research, it became obvious to me that the Kansas Harvey story should also be told. After all, Kansas *is* where it all began.

I am so thankful for the structure and organization of the Fred Harvey Company for—all these many, many years later—that has made it possible for me to tell this story. Many of the photographs that we have today to help pay tribute to the Harvey Girls and other Harvey employees are possible because of the company's careful photographic documentation. In the early years of the Fred Harvey Company, the Harvey staff photographer, Gay M. Hamilton, recorded the Fred Harvey history for us. Hamilton was also the official photographer for the *Santa Fe Employes' [sic]* magazine.

Lesley Poling-Kempes, author of *The Harvey Girls*, has said that her book emphasized "the historical importance of ordinary people." I'm using Lesley's words here to encourage anyone reading this book to recognize the importance of your family history, the story of your hometown—stories of ordinary people—and to begin to preserve that history.

It seems to me that in Kansas the railroad was efficiently hurrying across the state to travel farther west all the way to California, and the Fred Harvey Company was instrumental in making this happen. As the Santa Fe and Harvey Houses made their way across the Southwest—New Mexico, Arizona and California—Harvey catered more to tourists with an attitude of "stop and stay awhile." Kansas was the stable foundation for the innovative, visionary Fred Harvey Company.

Exact dates of when some Kansas Harvey Houses opened and closed have been difficult to verify. These dates are not always consistent between information in Fred Harvey Company archives and more recent publications. For the purposes of this book, I have primarily depended on an undated typed list of "Fred Harvey Operations" I found in the Fred Harvey

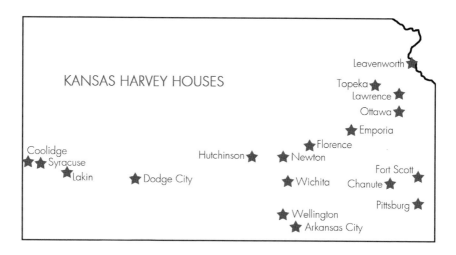

Harvey Houses in Kansas. *Map by Melissa Morrow.*

Collection of the Cline Library, University of Northern Arizona, for dates of operation. In some instances, this list did not give an exact date but rather had a notation such as "opened before 1915." When I encountered this, I used dates provided by a museum or library in the town where the Harvey House existed.

Certainly, Fred Harvey had a unique vision for restaurants along the railroad and was an astute businessman, as were his sons and grandsons who continued the business after Mr. Harvey's death. However, it was the employees, led by Harvey Girls, who made the Fred Harvey Company a success. I am pleased to share this history with you.

1

FRED HARVEY IN KANSAS

Where It All Began

Fred Harvey's narrative in the United States began when the teenage Englishman immigrated in 1850. Harvey learned the restaurant business working as a pot scrubber and busboy in New York. In July 1858, at the age of twenty-four, Frederick Henry Harvey became a U.S. citizen in St. Louis, Missouri. Later, he owned a café in St. Louis that catered to wealthy businessmen who expected fast service and good food served in tasteful surroundings. However, the effects of the Civil War and a dishonest partner brought an end to Harvey's first restaurant venture. He then found employment with the railroad as a freight agent, solicitor and mail clerk traveling many miles by rail. This experience provided firsthand knowledge of how difficult it was to get decent food while traveling by train, and this knowledge would serve Fred Harvey well.

Mr. Harvey knew the Santa Fe Railroad was expanding and needed to develop a robust passenger business to finance the growth. With his knowledge of the restaurant business, he believed he could help accomplish this. When Harvey met with Santa Fe officials in 1876, the entrepreneur was confident he could personally change the miserable reputation of railway dining and increase passenger service. On a handshake with the president of the Santa Fe Railroad, an agreement was reached, and the first restaurant chain in the United States was launched.

As Fred Harvey's chain of trackside restaurants grew, when a location was deemed appropriate for a Harvey establishment, the Santa Fe would design and build space in or adjacent to the new depot building for the kitchen, food

Fred Harvey, founder of Harvey House restaurants, newsstands and hotels. Harvey is credited for bringing a high standard of hospitality to towns along the Santa Fe Railroad. *Courtesy of kansasmemory.org, Kansas State Historical Society.*

storage, a lunch counter and usually a dining room, as well as living quarters for Harvey employees. This space, built especially for Fred Harvey's business venture, would be called a Harvey House. Mr. Harvey was also afforded the use of Santa Fe trains to deliver laundry, food products and employees along the line at no charge.

Originally, Harvey Houses were established along the railroad at intervals of approximately one hundred miles, providing dining opportunities for passengers when the train stopped to refuel the steam engine. Other sites

Kansas Harvey House staff. *Courtesy of Carolyn Rosser.*

were determined by the location of Santa Fe division points where large numbers of railroad employees needed a place to eat.

It is often stated that Fred Harvey civilized the West; however, I agree with Philip F. Anschutz's assessment of Harvey in his recently published book, *Out Where the West Begins.* Anschutz included Harvey in this volume of "profiles, visions and strategies of early Western business leaders," along with other notable businessmen such as Henry Ford, J.P. Morgan and Texas cattleman Charles Goodnight. The author writes that "Harvey's dining and tourism dynasty introduced the West to *new forms* of civilization, powerfully influencing our popular imagination to this very day."

Referring to the famous Harvey Girls, Anschutz wrote that historians "have noted how Harvey's hiring practices represented an important opportunity for single young women. Not since the beginning of the Massachusetts textile industry in the 1820s had American girls seen such a chance to break away from their parents' control and make a living on their own."

The Fred Harvey company valued consistent food quality as much as quality of service. Only the best, freshly prepared food was offered at a Harvey House, and travelers soon realized they could trust the Fred Harvey name all along the Santa Fe line.

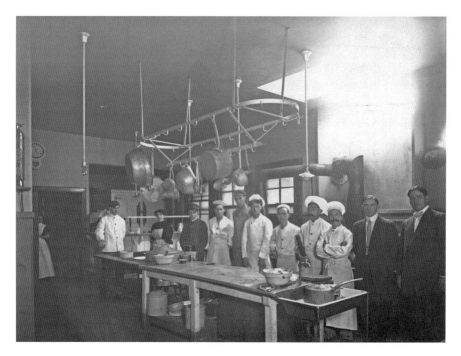

The kitchen staff and Harvey managers at the Sequoyah in Syracuse, Kansas. This was the first job in a long career with Fred Harvey for Earl A. Reynolds (fifth from right). Within two years, Earl became a chef and worked in Harvey Houses in Belen and Clovis, New Mexico. *Courtesy of Louise Reynolds and family.*

William Allen White, Pulitzer Prize–winning publisher of the *Emporia Gazette*, believed that Fred Harvey's food raised the standard for home-cooked food in America: "Men who have eaten at Fred Harvey's eating houses have come home and insisted on having their meats broiled, not fried; their roasts roasted, not boiled; their potatoes decently cooked and their biscuits light."

Harvey House managers were required to send tabulated reports to the Harvey headquarters in Kansas City, Missouri, at the end of each day. The purpose of these reports was not to assess possible ways of reducing expenses but to ensure that the Harvey standard was maintained. *Santa Fe* magazine explained that the reports made certain "the slices of ham in the Harvey sandwiches are as thick as ever and the same thickness everywhere and that the coffee is as strong as it should be." (This debunks an often-told Fred Harvey quote to his sons, "Cut the ham thinner," and supports those who reported his final advice as being "Don't cut the ham too thin.") In Harvey Houses, whole pies were cut into four servings instead of the usual six or eight in other restaurants. The daily reports reflected the inventory of food used in relation to the number of customers served, indicating whether portions were up to Harvey standards. Many Harvey Houses operated in the red for years. Fred Harvey's business philosophy was simple. He believed that profits would come in the long run if excellent service was provided and maintained.

The Harvey managers were often chosen from existing newsstand managers or cashiers. The Harvey system was set up much like that of the Santa Fe with the manager reporting to a superintendent in charge of a certain territory. In each territory, traveling inspectors and auditors were constantly inspecting the hotels and restaurants to ensure they maintained the Fred Harvey standard of service. The superintendent reported to the Harvey office in Kansas City. In the early days, Fred Harvey was often one of the traveling inspectors, and Harvey House staff had various codes used by train conductors to telegraph a warning that "the boss" was on the next arriving train.

In 1945, the Fred Harvey company reported that over 41 million meals had been served with a gross business of over $37 million, the largest in the company's seventy-year history. This large increase in business was primarily a result of the many thousands of meals served at Harvey Houses to troops who were transported by train during World War II. At the end of 1947, a *Holiday* magazine article titled "Englishman's U.S. Revolution" reported that the Harvey system covered "over 3000 miles from Cleveland to Los Angeles, and requires a staff of 7000 persons who include many a Harvey Boy as well as modern versions of the Harvey Girl."

Not only did Harvey Houses get their start in Kansas, but the Atchison, Topeka and Santa Fe (ATSF) line also began in the state. Originally founded in 1860 by businessmen from Topeka and Atchison, Kansas, due to the disruption of the Civil War, it was eight years before any track was put down. Almost four years later, the track reached Dodge City, three hundred miles west. Approximately twenty years later, the ATSF finally came close to, but didn't extend into, Santa Fe, New Mexico, as originally planned. The railroad civil engineers determined that the hills surrounding the town of Santa Fe were too steep for the engines of the time. The main line was instead built through Lamy, New Mexico, approximately eighteen miles southeast of Santa Fe. Later, a spur line was built into the city of Santa Fe.

Just before the turn of the twentieth century, Fred Harvey's restaurant and hotel business was prospering, and as the only railroad line offering this level of service to its passengers, the ATSF was experiencing an increase in profits, too. The railroad executives were so pleased with their Harvey

An early Harvey House at Syracuse, Kansas.

Harvey Girls and the Harvey manager in the late 1880s outside the original Harvey House, Syracuse, Kansas. *Courtesy of kansasmemory.org, Kansas State Historical Society.*

partnership that, in 1889, they granted Fred Harvey a "sweetheart contract," giving him the monopoly of all dining sites on the ATSF line. The railroad further agreed to transport all supplies and employees for no charge, as well as supply fuel, ice and fresh water to all Harvey establishments. It was also most likely that at this time or soon after, the railroad agreed to provide space on Santa Fe property rent free for Fred Harvey restaurants, hotels and employee living quarters.

Perhaps the most important provision granted Harvey in this contract was the exclusive right of food procurement west of the Missouri River. Fred Harvey was granted the exclusive right, with some minor reservations, to manage and operate the "eating houses, lunch stands, and hotel facilities which the company then owned, leased, or was to lease at any time in the future upon any of its railroads west of the Missouri River, including all lines then leased or operated in the name of the Atchison, Topeka and Santa Fe. Coal, ice, and water were to be provided by the railroad; employees and supplies were to be hauled free. Profits, arising from the operations were to go to Fred Harvey in full for all services rendered by him in such business."

That same year, a chain of events was begun that threatened the partnership between Fred Harvey and the Atchison, Topeka and Santa Fe.

Although the partnership between Fred Harvey and the railroad is generally portrayed as a congenial collaboration, after Allen Manvel became president of the ATSF in September 1889, he initiated plans for dining car service west of Kansas City. Fred Harvey was not part of this plan.

Two years later, Fred Harvey filed suit in Chicago attempting to restrain the Atchison, Topeka and Santa Fe Railway from running or operating dining cars along the line west of the Missouri River. The legal action stated that the ATSF had violated its contract with Harvey to supply passengers with meals in trackside restaurants by operating dining cars from Chicago to Denver. Harvey obtained an injunction enjoining the railroad company from interfering with his business and from refusing to stop at his eating establishments. He claimed that his restaurants had cost him over $100,000. An interesting note here: Judge W.C. Hook of Cook County, who granted the restraining order, was a close personal friend of Fred Harvey and served as an honorary pallbearer at Harvey's funeral.

The suit dragged on for several years, during which Manvel backed off from his ATSF dining car business plan. Soon after this breach in the "sweetheart deal" between Fred Harvey and the railway company, the ATSF went into receivership; however, even during this period, Fred Harvey prospered. After reorganization of the railroad company, then ATSF president Edward P. Ripley reached a contract agreement with Harvey that was finalized in 1899.

Soon, Santa Fe advertising began to tout its dining car service as being "under management of Mr. Fred Harvey."

There were other signs that Fred Harvey and the ATSF were "playing nice" again. To ensure that no passengers missed the train, it became common practice in the early 1900s for the train conductors to call departing trains in the depot waiting rooms—men's and ladies'—as well as in the Harvey House.

Harvey's special refrigerated boxcar was shuttled twice a week between Los Angeles and Kansas City, supplying Harvey Houses with California fruits and vegetables on the eastbound run and the best Kansas City meats on the return trip.

The Harvey organization centralized its menu selections. Menus were planned in four-day increments, printed in the Kansas City, Missouri office and distributed along the line in such a way that train passengers traveling

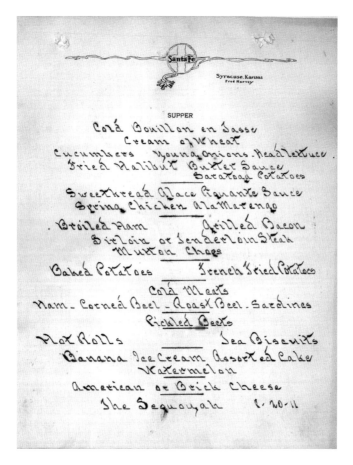

A hand-lettered menu for the Harvey dining room, the Sequoyah, in Syracuse, Kansas, August 20, 1911. Menu items were dictated from the Harvey offices in Kansas City. *Courtesy of Louise Reynolds and family.*

a long distance were presented with a variety of entree selections. In some locations, such as Syracuse, Kansas, the menu was hand-lettered on site but still followed the menu planned by the home office.

The July 1900 news story covering the newly completed extension of the Santa Fe route to San Francisco talks about the excellence of service provided by the ATSF through single ownership and management of the line. "Overland trains by this route do not miss connection because they run through." As was common, Fred Harvey was part of the ATSF story. "The eating-house and dining-car service is of the same superior quality throughout, under management of Mr. Fred Harvey. The best equipment is

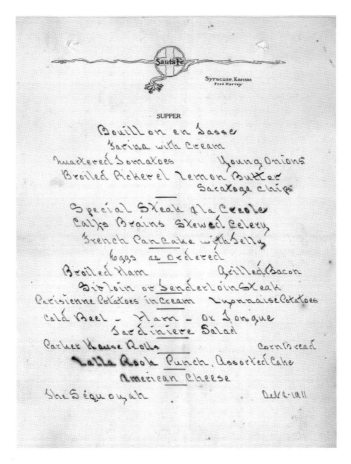

A hand-lettered menu for the Harvey dining room, the Sequoyah, in Syracuse, Kansas, October 8, 1911. *Courtesy of Louise Reynolds and family.*

provided. Employes [*sic*] are everywhere solicitous and courteous. Responsibility for the comfort of passengers is not divided."

Special heavy-roast Fred Harvey coffee was always a favorite of Harvey House customers. The company's annual report for 1907 showed 300,000 pounds of coffee were brewed that year. Fred Harvey coffee was also available to take home. The company marketing encouraged customers to do this by distributing printed instructions for brewing the best coffee: "The secrets of good coffee are that it be 1) made strong enough, 2) served hot enough, 3) brewed correctly, 4) always freshly made and 5) made from good coffee." Following these points, specific instructions were given on how to successfully make Fred Harvey coffee

Fred Harvey private label coffee was a favorite of Harvey House customers. The iconic Fred Harvey signature was used on all Harvey products, marketing pieces and signage. Some have credited architect and designer Mary Colter for transforming Harvey's actual signature into the company logo. Colter designed many Harvey Houses, as well as buildings at the Grand Canyon. *Photo by Beau Gentry. Courtesy of Skip Gentry's Fred Harvey Memorabilia Collection.*

at home, whether you prepared drip coffee or percolator coffee or used a glass coffee maker or an automatic coffee maker.

Fred Harvey was often described as high-strung and demanding. His strict rules for his employees, especially Harvey Girls, are well known. This set of rules posted in Harvey employee living quarters is dated 1887:

> *Employees are requested not to scratch matches, drive nails or tacks, or any other way mar the walls of their rooms.*
> *No rubbish of any kind must be thrown in the toilets.*
> *Bath tubs must be thoroughly cleaned by employes* [sic] *after using.*
> *Loud talking and laughing in rooms and halls should be avoided.*
> *Employes* [sic] *must be in their rooms by 11:00 o'clock p.m. unless given special permission by manager to remain out longer.*
> *Rooms must be kept in tidy condition and wearing apparel must be kept in its proper place.*
> *Expectorating on floors is positively forbidden.*
> *The purpose of the above rules is to bring about a tidy and homelike condition in your rooms and we request your co-operation so that the desired results will be brought about.*
>
> *Fred Harvey*

By the early 1960s, the Fred Harvey Company and its employee rules had, of course, changed considerably, as had travel and the experience of eating in a restaurant. Employees no longer lived under Mr. Harvey's roof. An employee manual distributed in the early 1960s contained standard information regarding vacations, payday, overtime pay and safety. However, the message in the first paragraphs of the manual is reminiscent of the early Harvey days when, many years after Mr. Harvey's death, employees still declared, "I work for Fred Harvey":

> *Each and every employee and the job he or she does is vital to the continued success of Fred Harvey and we are glad to have you with us. We want you to feel at home, to be happy in your work and to be glad that you have joined our family.*
>
> *Fred Harvey is known internationally for good food, for fine and friendly service and for the charm of our restaurants, shops and hotels. These basic principles were behind the founding of the first Harvey House in the railroad depot at Topeka, Kan., in 1876 and they are just as important now as they were in the beginning.*
>
> *Wherever one finds Fred Harvey…whether at Chicago's luxurious Kungsholm, at wonderful old El Tovar at the Grand Canyon, at the Pavilion in Los Angeles' Music Center or at the Oasis restaurants on the Illinois tollway…one finds the same spirit of hospitality and gracious service.*
>
> *Let's take just a minute or two to think about COURTESY. After all, courtesy or thoughtfulness and concern for others is the key to a successful relationship with our guests and with our co-workers.*

The front cover of this employee manual has an illustration of a family dressed in typical 1960s fashion exiting a Harvey House restaurant. The exterior of the restaurant looks very much like an orange-roofed Howard Johnson restaurant, a successful restaurant/hotel chain during the 1960s and 1970s. However, a section of the employee manual with "basic information for those of you who have joined the ranks of the world's most famous group of waitresses" is illustrated with a drawing of a Harvey Girl in a traditional, ankle-length black-and-white uniform. Almost a century after its inception, the Fred Harvey Company was still clinging to the positive public reputation of the Harvey Girl:

> *The success of the first Fred Harvey restaurant and of every other Fred Harvey restaurant since that time has been largely dependent upon*

the fine job done by these young ladies…or Harvey Girls as they have always been known.

You are the person who represents Fred Harvey to our guests. If they are pleased with you and with your service they are pleased with Fred Harvey. If they are unhappy with you there is very little the company can do about it.

It is no exaggeration to say that not only your own job but the success of the HARVEY HOUSE itself depends upon you.

Our guests will be interested in:

Your appearance

Your attitude

Your service

And if you do the sort of job that these guests have come to expect from a HARVEY GIRL, you will be rewarded in a number of ways.

Once the historical pride of the Harvey Girl had been established, a photograph of the 1960s Harvey waitress uniform with the hem coming just below the knee accompanied company rules about personal appearance:

Take pride in your appearance. Look professional in your grooming.

Bathe daily before coming to work and follow your bath with the application of an effective deodorant.

Wear fresh, clean lingerie.

Keep your hands and nails clean.

Be sure of a clean, sweet breath through proper daily care of your teeth and the use of a mouth wash or gargle.

Have clean hair, simply dressed and covered with a hair net.

Use make-up lightly, emphasizing a natural look.

Always take one last critical look in the mirror. Remember that a smile on your face is also a part of the Harvey Girl uniform.

While searching through old Kansas newspaper articles as research for this book, I began to realize that more often than not the writers in the early twentieth century did not use the term "Harvey Girl" to describe the young women who worked in the Harvey restaurants. Instead, they usually called them waitresses—a term generally avoided as the Fred Harvey Company developed its marketing. These early newspapers also usually referred to a local Harvey House as the "Harvey eating house" or "Santa Fe eating house."

A.T. and S.F. R.R. Depot, Chanute, Kansas.

Harvey Girls in front of the Santa Fe Depot and Harvey House, Chanute, Kansas. *Courtesy of Michael McMillan.*

The specifically worded classified ads that were an early call in northeastern publications for Harvey Girls were not necessary when local Harvey managers set about looking for employees. These ads also inform us that local women were being considered for the Harvey House. Brevity may have been a prime consideration to save on the cost of ads that appeared in the local newspaper such as: "Wanted—A pantry girl and waitress. Apply Harvey House, Santa Fe Depot."

Classifieds generally advertised for "good girls for waiters," "dining room girls wanted" or, perhaps after a flurry of Harvey Girl weddings, "Wanted—six waiter girls." A 1906 Newton, Kansas ad indicates that Harvey Girls were paid a little more than generally thought: "Wanted—Girls for railroad eating house service. Experience not necessary. Salary twenty dollars per month with board, room and transportation. For particulars apply in person at Harvey House, Newton." Occasionally, the ads for other jobs were less specific: "Good position for young industrious man of good habits. Good salary, room and board" and "Wanted—Man to take good garbage from Harvey House daily. See Manager." Another was seeking "a good, strong boy" to work as a porter.

Fred Harvey suffered from cancer for over fifteen years and died at the age of sixty-five in 1901. Fred Harvey Company documents show that same year

Harvey House staff, Syracuse, Kansas, soon after the Harvey House opened. The two head waitresses are wearing the traditional uniform of long, wraparound white aprons over black skirts and blouses; the other Harvey Girls are wearing black skirts and blouses with short white aprons. *Courtesy of the Hamilton County Historical Society.*

Mr. Harvey owned and operated fifteen hotels, forty-seven restaurants, thirty dining cars and a San Francisco Bay ferry.

This eulogy prepared by Elbert Hubbard, writer and publisher, was a sincere tribute to Mr. Harvey; however, looking back, we see it as an appropriate description of what the name "Fred Harvey" would mean for many years to come:

> *Fred Harvey? Do you know the name? If not, then your education has been much neglected. Fred Harvey used to run a restaurant. He ran it so well that the Santa Fe railroad folks got him to establish a line of restaurants along the road from Chicago to California, and also down into Texas. Some say that the Santa Fe made Fred Harvey, but the fact is, Fred Harvey had a little something to do with making the Santa Fe Railroad.*
>
> *Fred Harvey set a standard of excellence! It is a terrible thing to acquire a Fred Harvey reputation. Where the name, Fred Harvey,*

appears, the traveling public expects much. It may be on the desert of Arizona, a hundred miles from water, but if it is a Fred Harvey place, you get filtered spring water, ice, fresh fruit and every other good thing that you can find at the same season in the best places in New York or Chicago. How the miracle occurs you do not know—it is a Fred Harvey concern—that is enough!

And so this man, Fred Harvey, has educated thousands of young men and women, and showed them how to meet people, how to serve them without boring them, how to speed them on their way in gladness.

Fred Harvey is dead, but his spirit still lives. The standard of excellence he set can never go back. He has been a civilizer and benefactor. He has added to the physical, mental, and spiritual welfare of millions. No sermon can equal a Fred Harvey example—no poet can better a Fred Harvey precept. Fred Harvey simply kept faith with the public. He gave pretty nearly a perfect service. I did not know Fred Harvey, but I know this: he must have been an honest man, a good man—for the kind of business a man builds up is a reflection of himself—spun out of his heart. Man, like Deity, creates in his own image. I take off my hat to Fred Harvey, who served the patrons of the Santa Fe so faithfully and well, that dying, he yet lives, his name a symbol of all that is honest, excellent, hygienic, beautiful and useful.

After Fred Harvey's death, his sons, Ford and Byron, continued to operate the substantial family business and were very successful in expanding it. The decision was made for the company name to be simply "Fred Harvey," maintaining the illusion that the founder was still alive. For years after Mr. Harvey's death, employees continued to say they worked for Fred Harvey; in correspondence and printed marketing pieces, the company was referred to as "Fred Harvey."

Ford Harvey attended school in Leavenworth, Kansas, and it is believed that he left Racine College in Wisconsin after three years because of his father's failing health and began working in the Harvey company's Kansas City, Missouri offices. Ford had a variety of responsibilities and learned his father's business well. There was some speculation that Ford Harvey, who was appointed president of the company after his father's death, may have chosen the company name because of a lack of self-confidence. However, with experience from working beside his father for many years and a decisive manner of conducting business, I'm inclined to believe Ford realized this would be a smart marketing tactic. And it was!

Almost fifteen years after his father's death, Ford was recognized for his "executive qualifications and business ability" by the Missouri newspaper the *Independent*:

> *Ford P. Harvey leaves an eighteen carat hall mark on his record as a business man. Since his elevation to the head of the great Harvey system its expansion and growth has been of the most stable and progressive character. The achievements of his father have been doubly complimented by respectful acknowledgement, and by a continued uplifting of standards. In fact, the regime of the Harvey system, under the son's presidency has been a question of ideals. Ford Harvey is peculiarly lacking in personal ambition. Even his identity is obscure to the general public to whom only the name Fred Harvey is familiar. And he has lost sight of ambition for the great big successful business which he operates in his determination to make and keep it at the highest possible standard.*

Fred Harvey's sons established separate offices with Ford in Kansas City and Byron in Chicago. During this time, Ford was responsible for hotels, restaurants, newsstands and shops, and Byron managed the railroad dining cars.

Until the end of the nineteenth century, Harvey Houses were of inexpensive frame construction and built for efficiency. In the early 1900s, Ford Harvey and Santa Fe president Edward P. Ripley began to consider building new railroad depots and Harvey establishments reminiscent of the Spanish Colonial–Indian pueblo style of architecture. The men agreed on a plan that called for construction of a system-wide series of approximately twenty trackside hotels, some of which would be regional in design. The railroad architects would continue to participate in the design of the new buildings; however, others, such as Louis Curtiss of Kansas City, were commissioned to design the buildings and to supervise construction.

In an interview shortly before his death in 1928, Ford explained the difficulties of operating Harvey Houses:

> *With us it is the task of seeing to it that every long-distance passenger upon the railroads that we serve has proper food accommodations for the entire duration of his journey. We have to meet the tastes and whims of all sorts and conditions of men—those to whom a trip across the continent is ordinary routine, and those who are on a train for the first time. I have found the most-traveled man makes the least fuss about what we serve him.*

The Arcade Hotel, Newton, Kansas, was built in 1900 at the intersection of Main Street and the railroad tracks. *Courtesy of Michael McMillan.*

It is the untraveled person who is apt to be the most exacting. Yet he or she is entitled none the less to the very best service that we can possibly render.

A man may have only thirty cents to pay for a meal, but we must treat him with the same deference and courtesy as if he were paying ten times that amount. He may not tip the waitress in the lunchroom. That often happens. It is our business, however, to keep that employe [sic] just as well satisfied as if he had received a generous tip, so that the next time that man comes over the road—our people have an uncanny way of remembering and of recognizing them—they will render him just as good service as if he had established a reputation along the line as a generous giver.

We create the very best working conditions—wages, hours, surroundings—that we can possibly devise for our people, by working with them all the time, never letting them remain in the dark as to our plans or as to our methods, and then by letting them feel that the hotel or restaurant of which they may be in charge is, for the time being at least, theirs, not ours.

Following Ford's death, Byron Harvey became president of the Fred Harvey Company and continued in that capacity until his death in 1954.

There are many letters in various Fred Harvey Company archives written by satisfied customers through the years. Often, Ford or Byron Harvey would circulate copies of the letters to Harvey managers urging them to carry on the company's standards. According to an article in the *Santa Fe Employes'* [*sic*] magazine in 1910, the following letter written by H.R. Pattengill of Michigan was quoted in the editorial columns of a number of western newspapers:

> *Nearly forty days of travel and experience along the Santa Fe, and corresponding familiarity with the Harvey eating-house system, leads us to pay this tribute to its force of dining-room girls. In all this time, in a score of different hotels, and of the hundreds of waiters, the editor did not see any unladylike or flippant action. The young ladies were, without exception, neat and becomingly attired, courteous and expert in their work, dignified yet cheery, bright eyed, clear faced and intelligent. It is also worthy of note that they received from the thousands of guests whom they served the courtesy which their bearing demanded. Some of the traveling show troupe women, with their bepowdered, enameled, ready-made complexions, peroxide puffs, wienerwurst curls, loud talk and louder behavior, might well get some wholesome lessons in womanliness from the Harvey House waitresses.*

Ahead of its time, the Fred Harvey Company was establishing its brand over a century before "branding" became a buzzword. Fred Harvey fruit preserves were served at breakfast. For a time, Coca-Cola bottles produced in Newton, Kansas, had the imprint "Fred Harvey Newton" on the bottom. Harvey Houses are credited with originating the "blue-plate special," a daily low-priced complete meal that was served on a blue-patterned china plate. An 1892 Harvey menu mentions this dining option some thirty years before it became a common restaurant term. In the United States, until the early 1960s, when the country's eating habits began to change, ordering the blue-plate or daily special in a café or diner meant you got a meal predetermined by the restaurant, usually consisting of meat, vegetables and bread served on one plate for a reduced price.

The Fred Harvey logo, composed simply of Mr. Harvey's signature, was attached to high-quality products such as coffee, whiskey and cigars, as well as menus and signage. Some have credited Mary Colter for transforming Harvey's actual signature into the company logo. An architect who had a long career with Fred Harvey, Colter designed many Harvey Houses, as well as buildings at the Grand Canyon.

Whenever possible, the Fred Harvey Company encouraged publicity about its food and hotel service with the use of well-placed newspaper and magazine articles. An often-used phrase was that Fred Harvey set the desert abloom

This aluminum sign announcing dinner was used in the remaining Kansas Harvey eating establishments in the 1950s and on railway dining cars. *Photo by Beau Gentry. Courtesy of Skip Gentry's Fred Harvey Memorabilia Collection.*

with beefsteaks. A 1940s article printed in the *American Mercury* magazine and reprinted in *Reader's Digest* cleverly described Fred Harvey as "turning a shoestring potato into a 2,500-mile string of railroad eating places." The article also said that Harvey "unconsciously launched a 'matrimonial bureau' which played a major role in civilizing the Southwest." All along the route of the Santa Fe, "you can talk with fine young college men and girls who are proud that Mother once worked for Fred Harvey and met Dad over the pie counter."

The decline in Harvey Houses beginning in the 1930s has been attributed to several factors. One is the increase in the number of dining cars, allowing passengers to enjoy delicious, well-prepared meals in comfortable surroundings without leaving the train. Even in the late 1800s, Fred Harvey's dining car service was competing with his trackside restaurants. In the fall of 1897, the ATSF announced that the fast California limited train would resume its service. The passenger train would make the run through Kansas across the country to Los Angeles in fifty-four hours. Described as a "hotel on wheels," passengers had dinner in Kansas, breakfast in Colorado, lunch in New Mexico, dinner the second day in Arizona and breakfast and lunch in California. A first-class, one-way ticket was thirty dollars (meals not included).

The Sequoyah Harvey House, Syracuse, Kansas. *Courtesy of Louise Reynolds and family.*

Years later, the Fred Harvey restaurant system had to move to where most passengers went: airports and resorts. In 1968, the company supervised food service on the dining cars of the Santa Fe Railway in an operation that extended over thirteen thousand miles of railroad track. Many Harvey locations had closed, but railroad stations such as Chicago's Union Station remained important because of a concentration of commuter traffic. A company report stated that approximately a dozen Harvey restaurants and gift shops were still operating at that time.

The Fred Harvey Company became a subsidiary of Amfac, Inc. in 1968. To some extent, the Harvey influence remained intact with Daggett Harvey Jr., great-grandson of Fred Harvey, and Stewart Harvey, grandson of Fred, serving on the Amfac board of directors for a time. Of course, many things changed, and this transaction was not well received by former Harvey employees who had been loyal to Fred Harvey. Opal Sells Hill, a Harvey Girl veteran of forty-five years, recalled, "When Amfac took over Harvey, everyone was told, 'Throw out them Harvey Girl uniforms.' And they did. What a shame."

Through a merger in the early 1990s, all that remained of the Fred Harvey Company—El Tovar and Bright Angel Lodge at the Grand Canyon—became part of Xanterra, the largest parks concession management company in the United States. On its website, www.xanterra.com, the company refers to the Fred Harvey Company's proven expertise and Xanterra's commitment to those principles in today's hospitality business.

2

HARVEY GIRLS

Challenging Stereotypes

As Mr. Harvey's vision for first-class eating establishments along the Santa Fe Railroad became a reality, there were challenges, the most predominate being the difficulty of finding employees who would maintain the Harvey standards.

In the small railroad towns, the population didn't provide many folks to consider. The prevailing story of how the idea of Harvey Girls unfolded takes place in Raton, New Mexico. In the early 1800s, when a Harvey House was established in this remote northern New Mexico town, an all-male staff served the eating house patrons, consisting mostly of miners, cowboys and railroad men. Following an after-hours fight involving the staff, no one was able to work the next morning. When word of the situation reached Fred Harvey, he took the train to Raton to remedy the situation. An enraged Harvey fired everyone and hired a new manager, Tom Gable. Gable proposed replacing the disorderly men with attractive young women, correctly reasoning that the women would be more reliable and cause less trouble. He believed the change in staff would also be well received by train passengers and the community. Harvey agreed. Using popular women's magazines and newspapers, he placed ads such as this to entice qualified young women to apply to work for Fred Harvey: "Wanted—Young women, 18–30 years of age, of good character, attractive, and intelligent, as waitresses in Harvey Eating Houses on the Santa Fe Railroad in the West. Good wages, with room and meals furnished. Experience not necessary. Write Fred Harvey, Union Depot, Kansas City, Missouri." Kansas Harvey House history, however, lists

Kansas Harvey Girl Dott Rohlin. *Courtesy of Carolyn Rosser.*

women, including a Harvey relative, as waitresses, as early as 1880, two years before the Raton incident.

Thousands of ambitious young women who passed the rigorous personal interview at the Kansas City, Missouri or, later, Chicago, Illinois Harvey offices were given a train pass to their new jobs and often left immediately. Some were sent home and weeks later received a letter on Fred Harvey stationery requesting that they report to work. Harvey Houses in Kansas were often staffed with local women who worked beside well-traveled, experienced Harvey Girls who had served in New Mexico and Texas.

The company accepted only women who presented themselves well—neatly dressed and groomed—and who spoke clearly and showed good manners. Harvey wasn't looking for experienced waitresses, as the company wanted to train its new hires in the strict "Harvey way." In the early years, all Harvey Girls were single and were required to sign a contract stipulating they would not marry during the first six months of employment. Between 1883 and the late 1950s, approximately 100,000 Harvey Girls proudly wore the now famous black-and-white uniforms.

The young women who answered Fred Harvey's classified ads did so for many different reasons. Some were simply looking for a way to leave the family farm and explore the possibilities of a different kind of life. Others realized the money they could make as a Harvey Girl would pay for the education required for a career in teaching or nursing. Some applicants were simply looking for adventure. Surely all the Harvey Girl hopefuls were keenly aware that working in a remote place where few women lived would

Harvey House lunchroom, Newton, Kansas. *Courtesy of kansasmemory.org, Kansas State Historical Society.*

provide opportunities for meeting a prospective husband. If somehow this possibility escaped a young woman, newspaper and magazine articles often emphasized this benefit with phrases such as "Sensible girls got their men by going where the men were."

Serving procedures were standardized throughout the Harvey system, and Harvey Girls usually had to train for a month before they were given their own tables or lunch counter seats to serve. In the beginning, the newcomers usually squeezed orange juice or cut the butter into squares, but soon they would be following another Harvey Girl and learning the proper way to interact with guests. The young women did not receive pay during this training time. If a girl couldn't meet the expected standards or decided that a Harvey Girl career wasn't what she wanted, she was given a train pass to go home.

Harvey Girls personalized the Fred Harvey standards and brought their eastern and midwestern sensibilities to a job that previously had not been held in high esteem. Harvey's strict rules about dressing modestly, wearing little or no makeup and conducting oneself in a respectable manner served

The entrance to the Harvey House dining room in the Santa Fe Depot, Newton, Kansas. *Courtesy of the Harvey County Historical Society.*

the purpose of reassuring the young ladies they would be in good company, working and living with likeminded women. Their reputations would be protected even far from home, where they would be judged without the benefit of a family's good reputation. In Newton, Kansas, in the early 1900s, the Harvey House manager designated a parlor on the third floor of the Arcade Hotel for the exclusive use of Harvey employees. This provided an acceptable place where Harvey Girls and their guests could meet socially.

At the time early Harvey Girls were hired, workingwomen were often scorned unless they were teachers or nurses. Waitressing in particular was considered one of the lowest professions a woman could choose and was certainly not a proper profession for a white, middle-class young woman. In the unsettled West, many waitresses were also prostitutes, and even when this was not true, the perception prevailed. Usually tough, coarse women were the only ones who could make it alone in remote, rural areas. The sheltered living circumstances provided for Harvey Girls made it possible for more refined women to survive in uncivilized, developing Kansas railroad towns where gunshots in the street were not uncommon.

Fred Harvey's rules were a dominant part of any Harvey Girl's experience, but they served many a good purpose. In addition to providing a protective atmosphere for the women, the rules standardized service in Harvey Houses and helped sell the Harvey ideal all along the Santa Fe. Just as Fred Harvey changed the standards for food and service for train passengers, he changed the standards for the job of a waitress. Harvey Girls were expected to conduct themselves in a ladylike manner at all times. This conduct changed the public perception of working, single women, especially waitresses.

An efficient, somewhat mysterious "cup code" helped streamline the service to harried train passengers. After diners were seated, a waitress would ask whether they preferred coffee, hot tea, iced tea or milk. She would then arrange the cup at the place setting before each patron and move to the next table. Soon, the "drink girl" would arrive at the table and magically pour the patron's

Unidentified Harvey Girls, circa 1910, in front of the Bisonte, Hutchinson, Kansas. *Courtesy of kansasmemory.org, Kansas State Historical Society.*

preferred drink without asking. If the waitress left the cup right side up in its saucer, that meant coffee; upside down meant hot tea; upside down but tilted against the saucer meant iced tea; and upside down, away from the saucer meant milk.

Getting dressed for work may have been the hardest part of the Harvey Girl job, as the uniform standards were exact and inspections frequent. The now familiar black-and-white uniforms were laundered at a Harvey laundry such as the one in Newton, Kansas, where restaurant and hotel linens were also sent. One Harvey Girl informed me, "The uniforms would come back clean and starched. All we had to do was iron them. I was living in the lap of luxury!" For many years, a hairnet and a corset were required,

A canvas laundry basket used to ship Harvey Girl uniforms and table linens by train from all Kansas Harvey Houses to the Harvey laundry facility in Newton, Kansas. Photo by Beau Gentry. *Courtesy of Skip Gentry's Fred Harvey Memorabilia Collection.*

and stiff white collars were attached to the uniform blouse with straight pins made invisible with white pin heads. Surprise inspections were not unusual—the skirt length measured, fingernails checked and, in the early years, verification that a corset was in place. Through the years, as Fred Harvey's business practices have been scrutinized, some have speculated that the use of pin fasteners on the Harvey Girl uniform rather than buttons further promoted the ideal of—to use a current phrase—teamwork. Even this small detail further established the need to work together to accomplish job responsibilities and, along with dormitory-style living accommodations, helped foster an attitude of camaraderie among the young women.

Some historians interpret the crisp black-and-white Harvey Girl uniforms as a way of ensuring a standard of decorum and service. Others believe Mr. Harvey chose the style to imitate a nun's habit, thus protecting the reputation of the young waitresses. Perhaps the uniforms were meant to remind patrons of a nurse's uniform, which would help establish a perception of professionalism and service. It is possible that by dressing the young women alike, distractions were eliminated and restaurant guests were more likely to be impressed by the exacting service and delicious food.

Harvey Girls and chambermaids at the Bisonte, the spacious Harvey hotel and restaurant in Hutchinson, Kansas. *Courtesy of kansasmemory.org, Kansas State Historical Society.*

Harvey Girls have been assigned the reputation of having civilized the rural towns where they worked through their contributions to church and community activities. Often, a new Harvey Girl would come from poor rural circumstances, yet she would introduce a love for reading or artistic talent to her adopted home. Many farm girls who became part of the Harvey family were thrust into a world where, for perhaps the first time, they were encouraged to be feminine and take pride in their appearance. The transition was easy to accomplish in the clean surroundings of the Harvey Girl living arrangement with plenty of hot water, some privacy and a dresser with a mirror.

When Harvey Girls and other Harvey employees reminisce about their years with Fred Harvey, invariably they describe the experience as being part of a large family. The girls helped one another through bouts of being homesick or a romance turned sour. Harmless pranks were frequent, especially when a fresh-faced, naïve Harvey Girl in training showed up behind the lunch counter. When oysters on the half shell were on the menu, the new girl would be told by an experienced Harvey Girl that once the oyster dish was cleared from the table, the shells had to be thoroughly washed and saved to be used again. Once the unsuspecting girl began scrubbing an oyster shell, someone would let her in on the joke.

At the time Fred Harvey handpicked waitresses; dressed them in proper, starched uniforms; and sent them out to feed the traveling public, I am not sure he realized how Harvey Girls would change the course of women's history. Many were the first to venture more than walking distance from their hometowns. Most were the first women in their families to work—to take on a role other than wife and mother. Parents, especially mothers, didn't understand why their daughters chose this strange, perhaps dangerous, new path. Harvey Girls earned wages for the first time in their lives, allowing them to save for an even brighter future or send money home to help a family struggling through the Depression. The attitude back home probably became more anxious when, after six months or a year, parents received a letter announcing marriage to a Santa Fe brakeman or a local rancher.

In her book *More Than Petticoats: Remarkable Kansas Women*, author Gina Kaufmann included a chapter in tribute to Harvey Girls. I think it is very appropriate for Kansas Harvey Girls to be honored alongside Kansas natives such as evangelist Carry Nation, classical composer Nora Holt, foreign war correspondent Peggy Hull and celebrated pilot Amelia Earhart.

3

HARVEY GIRLS AT THE MOVIES

Feisty Musical

As I chose the title for this chapter, I realized that if you are reading this book and you have seen the 1946 MGM movie *The Harvey Girls*, you probably didn't see it on the large screen at a movie theater. Instead, you most likely have enjoyed the delightful musical on a classic movie television channel. However, for the purposes of this book, let's envision how it must have been to watch popular celebrities of the time—Judy Garland, Ray Bolger and Angela Lansbury—in a feisty musical on the big screen while enjoying a bag of popcorn. The movie was based on the book by Samuel Adams and told the story of young, bold women who came west to be Harvey Girls.

When the movie made it to big screens across the country, theatergoers were introduced to the story of the Harvey Girls with these words: "When Fred Harvey pushed his chain of restaurants farther and farther west along the lengthening tracks of the Santa Fe, he brought with him one of the first civilizing forces this land had known: the Harvey Girls. These winsome waitresses conquered the West as surely as David Crockett and the Kit Carsons—not with powder horn and rifle but with a beefsteak and a cup of coffee."

The most memorable song in the movie is probably "On the Atchison, Topeka and the Santa Fe" with lyrics by Johnny Mercer and music by Harry Warren. In an interview, Mercer explained that he had seen the name of the railroad on a boxcar and thought it had a "nice, lyrical quality to it." After signing to write the music for the Harvey Girl movie, Mercer suggested a song

Publicity photograph for the 1946 movie *The Harvey Girls*, featuring Judy Garland. *Author's collection.*

about the railroad. After he had Warren's music, Mercer said he went to work on the words: "It was an easy one to write. As I recall, it took me about an hour." The song earned an Academy Award for Best Song.

The "train" song continues to be familiar after all this time; however, my favorite Mercer/Warren song in the movie is "The Train Must Be Fed," with lyrics that emphasize the high level of service expected by Fred Harvey. Garland sings about the perfection of Harvey Girl uniforms, perfection in the dining room and in Harvey Girl living quarters and "perfection in the way we feed the trains." This last line, of course, refers to the passengers who found their way from passenger trains into the trackside Harvey Houses to enjoy a meal served with Fred Harvey perfection.

The conservative, traditional Fred Harvey Company was originally opposed to the making of the Harvey Girl movie. Byron Harvey Sr., president of the company at the time, turned away a scout from a major California studio, expressing concerns about how his company and its Harvey Girls might be portrayed on the big screen. Months later, Byron was approached by a representative of Metro-Goldwyn-Mayer. A draft of a script was provided that met Byron's tentative approval. He

Sheet music of the Oscar-winning song "On the Atchison, Topeka and the Santa Fe," sung by Judy Garland in the 1946 MGM movie *The Harvey Girls*. *Photo by Beau Gentry. Courtesy of Skip Gentry's Fred Harvey Memorabilia Collection.*

was given assurance that the Fred Harvey Company would be allowed to approve each phase of the production. The MGM movie scout also brought a musical score and a singer to the Chicago Harvey offices. One version of the story describes the scene: "A delegation of Harveys accompanied the Metro man to a piano at the Blackstone Hotel on Michigan Avenue. There the singing of the score—especially the catchy *Atchison, Topeka & Santa Fe*—disolved [*sic*] all objections."

Actually, the musical, released almost seventy years ago, evolved into an extremely clever Fred Harvey marketing tactic. Ongoing correspondence between Metro-Goldwyn-Mayer Pictures and the Fred Harvey Company reveals the strong influence the Harvey executives tried to wield on advance publicity for the movie as well as the movie itself. To help appease the Harvey family, Byron Harvey Jr., grandson of Fred Harvey, was brought to

California as a technical adviser and was given a cameo role in the movie as a Santa Fe Railroad brakeman. A publicity photo was released showing the star of the movie, Judy Garland, with Byron Jr. and Byron Sr. all seated in movie director's chairs.

A Kansas native, Eleanor Bayler from Atchison appeared in the Harvey Girl film. You can easily spot her as the Harvey Girl who introduces Judy Garland before she sings "On the Atchison, Topeka and the Santa Fe" in the movie.

The Harvey Girls was declared one of the top movies of 1946 based on its gross earnings of $1.2 million. The national attention the movie would bring to Harvey Houses would certainly be a boon for business, but the reputation of the Harvey Girls had to be protected. In the fall of 1945, MGM began production on placards and other printed material to promote the January 1946 release of *The Harvey Girls*. Fred Harvey executives were not pleased. An October 1945 telegram from Byron Harvey Sr. to the MGM publicity department complained that the magazine and billboard advertising gave "the erroneous impression that this picture is largely a burlesque show or that the Harvey Girls were dance hall girls. In my opinion this type of advertising not only misrepresents the general character of the picture but is highly damaging to our company and its employees and is directly contrary to the spirit of our understanding."

Byron cited a letter he had written to MGM the previous year when he specified "that the production should be of such high quality that any publicity which the Fred Harvey system may derive from the picture will be of a favorable nature." Byron also stated that he had not seen the movie, but a Harvey company representative had tried to assure Byron, telling him "'the studio has sincerely tried to carry out our mutual understanding.' However, I feel very strongly that any favorable publicity our company and its employees may derive from the picture itself will be more than offset by such sensational advertising as is now apparently being produced."

Chief publicist and director of advertising for MGM, Howard Dietz, responded from his New York office: "I have gone over the ads and while we do use the dancing girl motif quite frequently it does not seem to be used offensively and is consistent with the idea of a musical picture." Dietz promised that "wherever possible in material not yet prepared we shall do our best to tone down what you consider objectionable and also attempt to make it clear that the Harvey Girls were not burlesque queens." With a conciliatory note, Dietz concluded: "I shall be extremely uncomfortable if you are dissatisfied with the treatment of the film and I want to do everything I can to find common ground."

Telegrams and letters between the two powerful men continued for some time, with Byron Harvey continuing to press his midwestern sensibilities on the New York publicity mogul. Harvey wrote that he found it "particularly objectionable" that Dietz's posters prominently featured "Alhambra [the saloon in the movie] girls with only minor picturization of Harvey Girls and with the wording 'The Harvey Girls' appearing opposite Angela Lansbury's legs." He went on to call the MGM advertising plan an "exploitation manual" and criticized proposed slogans for newspaper advertising. "If these slogans reflect your people's conception of the Harvey Girls picture I cannot help but feel deeply regretful for having given permission for this production. I hope you can send out one of your responsible assistants to show me other proposed advertising and to explain what steps are being taken to overcome my objections."

Byron Harvey also declined an invitation to come to New York for a screening of the Harvey Girl movie and stated, "I do hope you will decide to arrange a private showing for me in Chicago at an early date, as previously promised by your people in New York and Hollywood."

It may have been difficult for the Fred Harvey Company to bring New York and Hollywood up to its standards, but the Harvey home office maintained strict control over how publicity for the movie was handled in its establishments. Rigorous guidelines were provided to Harvey managers concerning promotion of the movie in Harvey Houses. Small posters were provided to all locations, and managers were told to attach them "on the bulletin board in the kitchen or fastened with gummed tape to the wall in a prominent location" so "your entire crew" will see them. The highly coordinated promotional message to the Harvey employees was, in Byron Harvey's words: "Millions are seeing *The Harvey Girls* on the screen and many of them will see us every day. Let's all be at our best!"

Large, freestanding cutouts of Judy Garland in a pristine black-and-white uniform were prominently displayed in Harvey House restaurants in towns where there was also a movie theater screening the Harvey Girl movie. Managers were instructed to acknowledge to the Fred Harvey main office that they received the cardboard figures and told to send an exact description of where the figures would be displayed.

The Harvey company also distributed special menus featuring promotional photos (without saloon girls) from the movie. Sent to Harvey Houses in December 1945, managers were instructed not to use them too far in advance of the premiere of the movie early the next year. During this time, the Harvey company also ran large ads in magazines with the headline,

Movie poster for *The Harvey Girls released in 1946.*
Photo by Beau Gentry. Courtesy of Skip Gentry's Fred Harvey Memorabilia Collection.

"What…a movie about us?" Always a marketing machine, Byron Harvey sent a reminder to managers: "In order for us to reap the potential benefits from this motion picture, it is necessary for us to have our house in order—standards of service, food, cleanliness, courtesy, and personnel at the very highest peak. We realize all this comes to us at a time when [we] are still very busy with the many problems left over from the war. Nevertheless we should grasp this opportunity and make the most of it. I am counting on all of you to do your very best to this end." The Fred Harvey Company was doing business, over forty years later, in the same way that Fred Harvey the man had done it before his death. And as originally intended, the attention to detail and service was a major windfall to train travel from Kansas to California as thousands traveled by rail knowing that Fred Harvey would take care of them.

Kansas movie houses sponsored contests to create interest in the Harvey Girl movie among the locals. The Granada Theater in Emporia had a contest asking readers to recount Harvey House incidents in letters to the newspaper. A winner was chosen each day of the week and awarded two guest tickets to *The Harvey Girls*. From the daily winners, one letter received the grand prize of a twenty-five-dollar war bond.

The release of the movie stirred memories of authentic Harvey House romances. The *Emporia Gazette* reported in its February 5, 1946 edition: "As the movie 'The Harvey Girls' continues to play to large crowds at the Granada Theater, stories about the Emporia Harvey House keep cropping up. One of the latest concerns the romance of Mr. and Mrs. Frank Girard, who live on a farm near Plymouth. Mr. Girard was chief chef at the opening of the Harvey House here and Mrs. Girard a Harvey Girl when they met and married."

A former Emporia Harvey Girl was one of the winners in the contest. Signing the letter "Mrs. Harvey Swint," the woman told about a dinner meeting of Santa Fe officials at the Emporia Harvey House: "A small band was playing and one of the girls started a rumor that I could do the 'Charleston,' a popular dance of the time. The men coaxed me to dance. I refused at first for fear I'd lose my job, but they guaranteed that I wouldn't. So I danced. Imagine my amazement when years after I was married I learned that the Harvey House manager was furious and that I would have been fired had not one of the Santa Fe head officials intervened."

Real Harvey Girls didn't sing and dance as much as Judy Garland did in the 1946 movie, but they worked hard, had some fun along the way and made Fred Harvey proud. All these decades later, we are proud, too, and thankful that thousands of women took a path away from familiarity and made life better for folks across the state of Kansas.

4

HARVEY HOTELS

Stay Awhile

COOLIDGE

The Santa Fe Railroad moved a division point to Coolidge in far southwest Kansas in 1881, and the town began to grow. Within five years, the population reached 1800, and there were three lumberyards, three dry goods stores, five eating places, seven grocery stores and an opera house. Several newspapers were established. In 1886, the same year Coolidge was incorporated, a large roundhouse was built, and a Harvey House was erected using the material from the former Lakin, Kansas Harvey House building. At this time, the Santa Fe Railroad was funding a monthly payroll in Coolidge of approximately $8,000.

After several controversial elections to establish the county seat of Hamilton County, the U.S. Land Office proclaimed Syracuse as the permanent county seat. County records and office equipment were moved from Coolidge to Syracuse on November 16, 1888. The town of Coolidge never recovered from these events, and circumstances continued to deteriorate.

At the turn of the century, the Coolidge town government attempted to increase the taxes on railroad property. The railroad refused to acknowledge or pay the additional amount, and one day when a train stopped in Coolidge, residents chained the locomotive to the tracks in an attempt to collect the taxes. Santa Fe employees freed the engine, and the train left town. Soon after the incident, the railroad left town, too. The Santa Fe division point was relocated to Syracuse.

The two-story clapboard Coolidge Harvey House that had originated in Lakin was moved to Syracuse. The town named for Thomas Jefferson Coolidge, president of the Atchison, Topeka and Santa Fe Railroad, was no longer a thriving railroad town, and by 1910, its population had dropped to fewer than 250.

With a population now of fewer than one hundred, Coolidge is considered a ghost town by some. Still, it once was a thriving western town. An indication of some of the issues facing the early settlement is a city ordinance that, according to a website about rural Kansas tourism, still exists, prohibiting women from riding naked on horseback. The law was deemed necessary in the early, wilder days of Coolidge, when ladies of dubious character would strip off their clothes, run out to welcome arriving cowboys and ride into town with them. These same women would sometimes ride slowly through town still unclothed, shocking the townsfolk.

Before the Santa Fe and Harvey House abandoned Coolidge, it enjoyed the influence of one of the most successful Fred Harvey managers in the history of the company. William Fonash was commended in a 1919 edition of *Santa Fe* magazine for being the oldest manager in the Fred Harvey system, having worked for the company for eighteen years. Following a job interview with Fred Harvey general manager Daniel Benjamin in Kansas City, Fonash was sent to Raton, New Mexico, as a baker and pastry cook and then moved to the Harvey House in Palmer Lake, Colorado. A year later, he was promoted to Harvey House manager at Palmer Lake and then transferred to Coolidge. The Harvey company later put Fonash in charge of the Brownwood, Texas Harvey House, and he later worked in the Cleburne, Fort Worth and Galveston Harvey restaurants. William Fonash had the distinction of having taught more cashiers and managers than anyone "on the line" and was known as "Teacher of Managers."

EMPORIA

When the new Emporia Harvey House opened in 1907, the Newton, Kansas newspaper the *Evening Kansan-Republican* printed this small piece revealing the local Harvey House pride and competition: "Emporia is making a big fuss over the new Harvey House opened there last Friday night. It is about one-third the size and importance of the local Harvey House, the Arcade." Actually, although the Emporia Harvey building was

Harvey House, Emporia, Kansas. The dining room served 104, and the lunchroom had forty-four high-backed stools around the marble counter. There were seven guest rooms upstairs, most of which were used for Harvey employee housing. *Courtesy of Michael McMillan.*

smaller than the one in Newton, the Emporia building was considered more ornate and distinct in design.

The building was designed by architect Louis Curtiss, known as the Frank Lloyd Wright of Kansas City, in a Renaissance Revival style of architecture. The exterior of the building changed drastically when it was enlarged by virtually building a new building around the old in 1925. The elegantly appointed dining room served 104, and there were forty-four high-backed stools surrounding the marble counter in the lunchroom. There were seven guest rooms, most of which were used for Harvey employee housing. The Emporia Harvey House closed in 1937, and the structure was destroyed by fire in 1999.

Olive Winter Loomis grew up on an Arkansas farm, and like many young farm girls in the early 1900s, she dreamed of leaving the farm life behind and making a different kind of life for herself. Her options were limited, as she had no experience except helping on the family farm. Somehow Olive heard about a job at a dime store in Topeka, Kansas, and decided she would give it a try. The job lasted only a week, and Olive desperately searched newspaper want ads trying to find another job so she wouldn't have to return to Arkansas. She answered an ad for waitresses to work in Harvey eating houses, was hired and sent to Emporia to work. As a Harvey Girl, Olive worked ten-hour days, often seven days a week, wearing a hot, starched uniform and shared living quarters with another woman. Hard as it was at times, Olive thrived and worked for Fred Harvey for nineteen years.

Emporia Harvey Girl Harriet Cross shared her experiences for an oral history project at Kansas State Teachers College. She was born in 1895 near Hesston, Kansas, and graduated from high school there in 1916. At the time of the interview in 1972, Harriet and her husband, Elmer, had lived on their farm southwest of Emporia, Kansas, for twenty-four years.

Harriet began her Harvey career in 1925 in Newton. She had worked as a bookkeeper in the Murphy Hotel and Restaurant Company across the street from the Harvey House for seven years but had never been inside the Harvey House until she applied for work. "I never imagined what was in there. If you don't think that wasn't an eye opener when I stepped in there!" After working two years in Newton, she was transferred to the Emporia Harvey House, where she worked as head waitress for three years. "That wasn't a long time considering what people usually worked, but the Harvey business was then on its way out. They were cutting down, so they cut me off. Rather than ship out [to another Harvey location], I just quit."

Harriett described the Harvey House as having the best food in the United States. "They had the best of everything—it was out of this world!" She explained that in addition to cigars and magazines, the Harvey newsstands sold fresh fruit: "They had everything—plums, grapes, oranges, apples." The former Harvey Girl described how they made fresh Thousand Isle salad dressing. "They had fresh, good olive oil, and they'd take the yolks of eggs, so much salt, so much sugar and so much mustard, and they'd whip that up into mayonnaise; then they would take little green onion[s] and chop them fine, hard-boiled eggs and pickles." These ingredients were added to the mayonnaise with a little ketchup added to that mixture. "We served quarter heads of lettuce to each guest. We had these little salad dressing boats, and we'd pour it on for the guests ourselves. Oh, I tell you, the service we used to give them!"

"We had tables for eight for the train people, and at each place we had seven pieces of silverware," Harriett continued. "When we'd start serving, we'd bring in soup first—the crackers would be on the table. Then when they had eaten their soup, we'd take the soup plates away and bring in the dinner plates all polished and hot." She further explained the sophisticated Harvey serving procedure: "We'd set the dinner plates down, then bring in the food. The manager would bring the meat out on a platter and our potatoes and vegetables in a baker. When we had the plates set down we'd go to the corner [of the table] and serve the two at each corner." Harriett remembered that the Harvey Girls always had to say, "May I serve you?" If the diner wanted the offered dish, the waitress placed it on the plate. As head waitress, it was Harriett's responsibility to reprimand another Harvey Girl who, when in a hurry, would say, "Tatas? Tatas?" when serving baked potatoes. The head waitress also had the responsibility of setting the cups on the tables following the unique Harvey cup code so the other waitresses would know what drink each diner had ordered.

Even serving the bread and butter followed a specific procedure. "Plain bread was in trays already on the table, and butter was served on a small dish that matched the Harvey china used for the meal. Hot bread was brought to the table in a silver tray. A napkin—a foot square, pure linen napkins from Ireland—would be folded and set in the tray, and we'd put hot rolls in the folds [of the napkin]. Then we'd open up the folds and ask the guest if he wanted one."

"Evenings, the meal was a dollar and a half, but they got their money's worth," Harriett continued. "Uptown they could get their meals for twenty-five or thirty-five cents, maybe half a dollar. At the Harvey House, though, we served all meals in three courses. The first course would be either consommé or some thin soup, and if it wasn't that, maybe it was fruit cocktail or oyster cocktail. After that course, we served fish if they wanted it—fish on a little platter." Following the fish course, the main course of meat and vegetables was served. "We brought all our food in on big metal trays," Harriett said. "When we served train passengers, sometimes we had to carry as many as fifteen or sixteen bowls on a tray, and we had to hoist them up in the air and balance them." Each meal ended with a choice of desserts.

Harriett described the delicious relishes served on trays. "We had all kinds of olives—they were beautiful olives, ripe, green and stuffed; then we had those little green onions and radishes and little German pickles, celery—I don't know if that's all or not—but they certainly had their choice."

The routine job of a Harvey Girl meant serving train passengers, railroad employees and local residents—usually ordinary folks; however, occasionally their work brought them in contact with well-known politicians and celebrities. In 1922, when the famous Russian soprano Oda Slobodskaja arrived at the Emporia Harvey House, it was obvious she was not an ordinary train passenger. On tour with the Ukrainian National Chorus, Slobodskaja was traveling to Tulsa, Oklahoma, when she entered the restaurant followed by the conductor carrying her luggage. Newspaper accounts of the visit described the soprano as "easy to look at and interesting to watch, but having no knowledge of the English language." She kept several waitresses at the Harvey House busy and was later turned over to the Santa Fe stationmaster to see that she was placed on train No. 201 on its arrival, more than an hour late. The soprano was "quite ill at ease during her stay. She would powder her nose, then retouch her lips with a red pencil, then adjust her oxford buckle, after which she would take a walk in the station and look at the clock and the train board."

John Brady, who had grown up near Emporia, worked as a busboy in the lunchroom at the Emporia Harvey House in the mid-1920s. One of his responsibilities was to ring the gong in front of the restaurant so train passengers could easily find their way. John also remembers making coffee early in the morning, polishing the brass railings on the counter and mopping the floor. He was also responsible for delivering box lunches to the black porters and conductors, as they were not allowed in the Emporia restaurant. The busboy was not to be seen in the restaurant while meals were being served; however, as soon as the passengers were back on the train, John began cleaning the floor while the Harvey Girls cleaned the counters. The exact routine was followed with each trainload of diners. "We served four trains a day—two at noon and two in the evening." Often celebrities would come through Emporia en route from Chicago to Los Angeles. "Local folks used to come down and watch to see who got off. Shirley Temple, Will Rogers, Jackie Cooper, Gloria Swanson and many, many more were seen on the Emporia platform."

Most Emporia Harvey employees were Kansas natives except the chef, baker and manager. Accommodations for Harvey employees in Emporia were upstairs, with Harvey Girls on one end and Harvey Guys on the other. Busboy John Brady recalled that in spite of close scrutiny of the manager and an 11:00 p.m. curfew, employees enjoyed their work and living arrangements. "We all became great friends at the house, but if the manager thought one of the guys was interested in one of the girls, well, it was a 'no-no.' I worked seven days a week and made thirty-five dollars a month plus room and board."

While researching Harvey Houses, I often hear stories about a chef or a baker making "homebrew" in the bathtub. Usually men from Europe were hired for the jobs of chef and baker, and perhaps the beer-making abilities were just one of the many skills these men brought with them. The Emporia version of the story is that the beer was consumed straight from the bathtub before it could be bottled. Before long, the smell permeated the upstairs and drifted into the restaurant downstairs. Following complaints from customers, the manager investigated and shut down the operation.

In 1890, Fred Harvey purchased a ranch of approximately eight hundred acres about ten miles southwest of Emporia. This was Harvey's initial venture into providing a source of fresh produce and meat for Harvey Houses, and the ranch was also a favored retreat for Fred Harvey. The *Emporia Gazette* reported that at this ranch, Harvey "raised immense crops of corn with which to fatten the big red steers grazing on luscious bluestem in nearby pastures, which when slaughtered provided the delectable steaks and roasts and soups for Harvey House customers along the Santa Fe system from Chicago to Los Angeles."

The design of the house Harvey built on the ranch property was very similar to the much larger Montezuma Harvey Hotel built in Las Vegas, New Mexico, a few years earlier. The two-story ranch house with a large wraparound porch provided plenty of space for the ranch foreman and his family to live full time and for the Harvey family, who visited often. The *Gazette* described the ranch house as having fourteen rooms, "a bath, closets, halls, pantries and storerooms, all built for comfort and convenience and luxurious living. Water was piped from a supply operated by a windmill." Although the house may have been considered luxurious for the time, living and working on the Harvey ranch was demanding. The *Gazette* article reported that Mr. Harvey paid Mr. and Mrs. James Troastal thirty-five dollars a month for the services of both. Mr. Troastal oversaw ranch operations, and his wife "had no help in the house, which always was kept in spotless order against the coming of the Harveys." Mrs. Troastal was responsible for "three-times-a-day big meals for a gang of husky cowboys and field hands" and eventually "felt she must be in better surroundings. She quit, and of course Mr. Troastal had to quit with her." Fred Harvey offered the couple fifty dollars a month to stay on the ranch and promised to hire a girl to help Mrs. Troastal, "but Mrs. Troastal declared she was through and never would take the job again."

In a letter to the *Emporia Gazette* in 1946, Mrs. W.H. Jacobs shared a family memory about the Harvey farm. The letter was an entry in a contest sponsored by the newspaper during opening week of the Harvey Girl movie at the Granada Theater in Emporia. "From 1883 until 1903 my father was foreman for the Harvey ranch. Fred Harvey and son Ford owned the ranch and the family spent two weeks each summer at the farm, hunting and fishing. They were entertaining and appreciative of the things my family did for them." Mrs. Jacobs included a humorous quip made by Fred Harvey:

"When Mr. Harvey and family came home from a hunting trip in the woods one day, my father asked Mr. Harvey what they got. Mr. Harvey replied, 'Wet clothes and a hungry stomach.'"

FLORENCE

The Clifton Hotel in Florence was built in 1976 and operated by local residents until Fred Harvey purchased it in 1878. According to information on the nomination form for the National Register of Historic Places, Harvey paid $4,275 for the building and $1,000 for the furniture. The new owner retained the name Clifton Hotel but totally redecorated the building, establishing the Fred Harvey standard for overnight accommodations. Some reports credit Mrs. Harvey with personally traveling to England to choose the china and silverware. Others believe Harvey used long-established contacts to import the tableware and fine furnishings from Europe. Regardless of how it was achieved, the tradition of high quality and service began in Florence.

Harvey House Museum, Florence, Kansas. The museum is housed in a portion of the original Clifton Hotel building where Fred Harvey established his first hotel. *Courtesy of Michael McMillan.*

The linens for the thirty-two-seat dining room were furnished from John S. Brown and Sons of Belfast, Ireland, and this practice continued as long as there were Harvey Houses. The linens were made of an exclusive pattern to match the imported china, and Mr. Harvey originated the use of the oversized napkin (still used on some Santa Fe dining cars) to accommodate the gentlemen who tucked them into their waistcoats. The two-story building with clapboard siding sat in a wooded area and was lighted throughout with coal oil lamps. Large stone fountains sat on each side of the front entrance, and there were wraparound porches on each story. A year later, Harvey remodeled and enlarged the wooden structure. The first Harvey hotel was a success among railroad passengers and the townspeople.

In Florence, Harvey began his long-held policy of employing experienced chefs for his hotel restaurants by hiring a chef from the exclusive Palmer House hotel in Chicago. A salary of $5,000 surely made the move from a bustling city to the small plains town of Florence, population one hundred at the time, an easy decision for the chef, who also served as general manager. (Note: in some writings it is reported that longtime Harvey chef Konrad Allgaier was first hired to run the Florence kitchen. However, Allgaier didn't come to the United

A Fred Harvey monogram marked silver serving pieces as well as china used in Harvey House dining rooms. Harvey's signature adorned the handles of all silverware. *Photo by Beau Gentry. Courtesy of Skip Gentry's Fred Harvey Memorabilia Collection.*

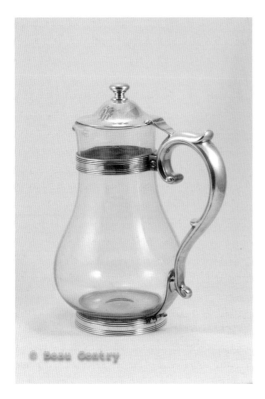

This silver and crystal water pitcher was used by Harvey Girls to serve guests in Harvey House dining rooms. Napkins and tablecloths were Irish linen. *Photo by Beau Gentry. Courtesy of Skip Gentry's Fred Harvey Memorabilia Collection.*

States from Germany until 1922, long after the Florence Harvey hotel closed. Allgaier worked as a chef on Fred Harvey dining cars until 1930, when he and his family moved to Santa Fe, New Mexico, where he became the chef at La Fonda Harvey House.)

The new, well-compensated chef at the Clifton Hotel in Florence began to purchase local food products, and farmers considered him an easy mark because he paid top dollar: $1.50 a dozen for prairie chickens, $0.75 for a dozen quail and $0.10 for a pound of butter. Mr. Harvey didn't quibble over the prices but always insisted that the chef buy the best.

During the first six months of 1879, over 2,300 guests stayed in the hotel. Harvey anticipated this increase in business, and in March, he enlarged the hotel and added a third-story tower over the main entrance. Some historians imply that Harvey had already made enough money from his Topeka lunchroom to establish the Florence location; however, others report that he received financial help from the Atchison, Topeka and Santa Fe Railroad.

One newspaper reported: "For fifty cents you can get all you want of the finest eatables money can buy." This included breakfast steak topped with fried eggs, potatoes, six-stack of wheat cakes with maple syrup, apple pie and coffee. Soon, four- and five-course dinner menus were offered for seventy-five cents. These included, on a rotating basis, a choice of sirloin of roast beef, capon, bluepoint oyster on the half shell, whitefish filet with Madeira sauce, pork loin with applesauce, roast duck, stuffed turkey, English-baked veal pie, sugar-cured ham with pickled lamb's tongue or prairie chicken with currant jelly. Half a dozen vegetables, a variety of salads and desserts such as pies, cakes, custards and cheeses were offered with the meat dishes, as well as coffee, tea or water.

Most days, eight trains passed through Florence with as many as fifty passengers on each one. Some meals at the Clifton were served family style at tables seating ten diners. There were also six smaller tables in the dining room. Four Harvey Girls handled meal service with three cooks in the kitchen and two chambermaids who helped during the busiest times.

According to information on the Florence, Kansas website, in the early days of this first Fred Harvey hotel and restaurant, four of the Harvey Girls lived in or near Florence. One of the women, Matilda Thomas, recalled that at sixteen years she was the youngest girl who worked at the Clifton. She personally met Mr. Harvey, who cautioned her not to throw the dishes so hard "or you'll break them." Matilda remembered that Harvey was "friendly and a nice man to work for."

Soon after the Florence hotel opened, a young widow with four small children moved to Florence from Illinois. She found a job washing dishes in the kitchen of the Clifton, and her oldest daughter was allowed to help her mother with the job. The girl was paid seventy-five cents a week, and her mother made seventeen dollars a month.

The Clifton Hotel was the scene of many local dances and special events and quickly became an important part of life in Florence, in a way you might not expect. In the summer of 1879, the following announcement appeared in the local newspaper: "Every Tuesday and Friday the ladies of Florence may have the use of the bathrooms at the Clifton Hotel...this will be a luxury which will be duly appreciated."

Other days, the bathrooms at the Clifton were open to gentlemen. For twenty-five cents, an individual could take a rainwater bath at the Clifton— quite a luxury for the time.

By the end of the nineteenth century, faster trains raced by the Florence Harvey House, continuing on to Newton. The last train passengers fed at this location was on the evening of March 31, 1900. The Clifton Hotel was closed later that year, and the large building was abandoned until 1904. The western section of the building was sold and moved to Main Street in Florence and established as the Price Hotel. One month later, another section of the Florence Harvey House was moved to Newton, Kansas. The original part of the hotel building was also moved, made into a rooming house and later used as a private residence. In the early 1970s, this building was acquired by the Florence Historical Society. The group maintains the building and, by appointment, offers tours and special dinners served by members in Harvey Girl uniforms.

DODGE CITY

A Kansas town with a reckless reputation, Dodge City was a center for buffalo hunters followed by an escalating cattle business. Both brought large numbers of transient people who fortified the economy but brought with them an unsettled, dangerous way of life.

Not long after the Atchison, Topeka and Santa Fe line reached Dodge City in 1872, the dusty, rough town was also the end of the trail for Texas cowboys who drove large herds of cattle north. From here, the livestock would be shipped by train to packinghouses in the East. In Dodge City, the cowboys got their pay for the long trip and were eager to have a good time before heading back to Texas. In 1884, railroad records reported over 800,000 head of cattle were put on ATSF trains heading out of Dodge City. The railroad welcomed the business, but generally life in Dodge City was

El Vaquero Harvey hotel, Dodge City, Kansas. The hotel had forty-one guest rooms, a lunchroom that served 47 and a large dining room that seated 118. *Courtesy of Michael McMillan.*

The spacious lobby of El Vaquero, the luxurious Harvey hotel in Dodge City, Kansas was a popular meeting place for businessmen. *Courtesy of kansasmemory.org, Kansas State Historical Society.*

not pleasant and often violent. Passenger train conductors carried guns to protect the money they collected for train fares out of Dodge City. The town's deputies, Bat Masterson and Wyatt Earp, earned their place in history by protecting town citizens and railroad property from rowdy cowboys at the end of a long cattle drive, as well as from miscreants who drifted in and out of town.

Fred Harvey's original Dodge City eating house—two boxcars, one for the kitchen and the other space for eating—opened in 1896. The outside might not have been especially inviting, but the inside was tastefully decorated in typical Harvey fashion, and of course, the food was delicious and well prepared.

The Harvey El Vaquero hotel opened in 1900, bringing a note of sophistication to Dodge City. The two-story building featured rounded arches, recessed entrances and accents of rough-cut stone that contrasted with the red brick of the structure. The impressive furnishings for the hotel were accumulated and stored in Newton beginning two years before the Dodge City hotel was completed. The hotel had forty-one guest rooms, a lunchroom that served 47 and a dining room that seated 118. This notable

Early Harvey House staff, Dodge City, Kansas. *Courtesy of Depot Theater Group, Dodge City, Kansas.*

structure certainly captured the attention of train passengers riding through early Kansas.

A total renovation of the building that contained the Santa Fe Depot and Harvey House El Vaquero hotel was accomplished in 1913. The significantly enlarged building occupied almost two blocks, making it one of the largest Harvey establishments of the time. The forty-five-thousand-square-foot facility would meet the increased demand caused by completion of the Dodge City–Colmar cutoff that extended southwest of Dodge City in an area that previously had no railroad service. The cost of the project was estimated to be $40,000.

During a summer road trip in 1915 from Dearborn, Michigan, to San Francisco, California, Edsel Ford, only child of Henry Ford, and six boyhood friends stopped in Dodge City and spent the night at El Vaquero. Driving a Ford Model T, the group has been credited with the making the first automobile road trip simply for pleasure. An interstate road system was just developing, and the group of young men used the National Old Trails Highway to eventually reach the Panama-Pacific International Exposition in San Francisco. Four years later, at age twenty-five, Edsel Ford would become

Large sun dials in Santa Fe Park adjacent to El Vaquero Harvey hotel, Dodge City, Kansas. *Courtesy of Michael McMillan.*

president of the Ford Motor Company. It would not be long before the popularity of the automobile would make car travel a strong competitor for passenger trains and the Harvey House system.

Hazel Williams went to work as a Harvey Girl in 1918, when she was fifteen. She, like quite a few other future Harvey Girls, lied about her age during an interview with the Harvey House manager. Hazel had grown up on a farm in Kansas and was ready to make a life of her own. She rode the train to Dodge City, where her older sister lived, and once she was hired, Hazel moved into the Harvey Girl living quarters. Years later, Hazel remembered being proud of how quickly she learned her job and how well she handled the rush of train passengers at mealtime. However, Hazel began socializing with a Harvey House busboy and was warned by the manager about the Harvey rule prohibiting employees from dating. She saw the young man one more time, and a housekeeper "tattled" to the manager. Hazel was given the option of moving to the Syracuse, Kansas Harvey House, but that would have taken her away from her family, so she declined the offer and was promptly fired.

According to longtime Harvey employee Opal Sells Hill, El Vaquero was not a favorite of Harvey Girls. "I worked in Dodge City in 1933 and there were lots of cowboys and cows. It was too wild for me and it was the only

Unidentified Harvey Girls, Dodge City, Kansas. *Courtesy of Depot Theater Group, Dodge City, Kansas.*

place that I ever asked for a quick transfer." Other Harvey Girls agreed, describing a hectic work schedule and no scheduled shifts. Trains arrived all hours of the day.

El Vaquero closed in 1948, and portions of the hotel space were used as railroad offices. In 1996, the Santa Fe donated the depot building to the city; it was placed on the National Register of Historic Places in 2000. The depot and Harvey House space currently houses an Amtrak passenger waiting area, meeting space and the Depot Theater Company.

HUTCHINSON

The city of Hutchinson was founded in 1871 when Indian agent Clinton "C.C." Hutchinson contracted with the Santa Fe Railway to make a town at the railroad's crossing over the Arkansas River. The community earned the nickname "Temperance City" due to the prohibition of alcohol set by its founder. Hutchinson was incorporated as a city in August 1872.

Construction of the new Santa Fe Depot and Harvey House in Hutchinson began in 1906 and was among the first designed to provide accommodations well suited for tourists. Harvey's Bisonte cost $250,000 and had eighty guest rooms. The restaurants could serve over 150, seating 110 in the dining room and 48 around the lunchroom counter. Other Kansas Harvey hotels built with this same purpose were El Vaquero in Dodge City and the Sequoyah in Syracuse. These hotels were operated on the European plan with rates beginning at $1.50 per day without bath and $2.00 with bath. Completed in 1908, the red brick building had a gabled roof punctuated with three large chimneys and a large, veranda-style porch. The structure was designed by nationally acclaimed Kansas architect Louis Curtiss in a style strongly influenced by the Arts and Crafts movement, especially the interior. The name—Bisonte, Spanish for buffalo—was appropriate for this site amid the windswept prairies of Kansas. The *Hutchinson News* reported that the hotel name was chosen by Santa Fe general manager Jim Hurley. A few years prior, Hurley had been a baggage handler at the Hutchinson station and was impressed by a great buffalo boneyard near the tracks waiting to be shipped away to become fertilizer. "Bisonte" was chosen as a tribute to the great buffalo herds but met with location opposition. Hutchinson community leaders favored a more sophisticated name, hoping it would entice more easterners to visit their town.

The formal opening of the Bisonte was celebrated with a public reception. Fresh flowers were scattered throughout, and music floated through the lobby and dining room. Guests were impressed by the tile and oak floors in common areas and thick carpets in the corridors and guest rooms on the second and third floors. Some guest rooms offered the luxury of private baths.

Almost every Santa Fe train that passed through Hutchinson would now be stopping for meals at the new Harvey House, and many train passengers would stay a while, enjoying a respite in the comfortable Bisonte accommodations. The Bisonte quickly became a popular post for Harvey employees. Harvey Girls especially considered a transfer to the Hutchinson restaurant akin to a

The Bisonte, a Fred Harvey hotel, Hutchinson, Kansas. Bisonte is Spanish for buffalo and was an appropriate name for the hotel built amid the windswept prairies of Kansas. *Courtesy of Michael McMillan.*

The impressive Bisonte lobby, Hutchinson, Kansas. This Harvey hotel was designed by well-known Kansas architect Louis Curtiss. *Courtesy of Michael McMillan.*

The dining room at the Bisonte in Hutchinson, Kansas. The luxurious hotel had eighty guest rooms, and the restaurants could serve over 150, seating 110 in the dining room and 48 around the lunchroom counter. *Courtesy of Michael McMillan.*

promotion or, at the very least, recognition by management that they were among the best waitresses.

An example of the size of the Hutchinson Harvey House and the efficient service it offered is a report of a large meeting held there in 1912 printed in a Chicago magazine:

More than 500 guests registered at the Bisonte hotel, Hutchinson, Kansas, during the industrial congress there. All were fed in the house and they who could not be given rooms under the roof were provided for at the Y.M.C.A., the Elks, and other quarters. It was a magnificent gathering of intelligent and well-bred men and women, and although, on account of the short recesses of the convention, the dining room was besieged at meal times, the proverbial order and politeness characteristic of the Fred Harvey System prevailed. The food came on without jar or confusion, and places were emptied and made ready for others with little delay. In addition, train meals were served on time.

Regularly at the noonday meals, 122 registered guests were seated, and the Harvey Girls served all without loss of time, or the infraction of anybody's patience. Great is the Harvey Girl! Directing the business, P.J.

Maguire, manager of the hotel, was commander-in-chief. Mr. Maguire is a veteran of the hotel business, and, properly, is the head of the Harvey system's largest and best equipped of the Santa Fe railway's long chain of hotels across the continent.

As the new era of train travel brought many easterners (as well as foreigners) west searching for new opportunities, Harvey hotels developed as a thriving center for traveling salesmen. Often called a "peddler" or a "drummer," the traveling salesman was also known as a commercial traveler. Over seven thousand people identified themselves with this occupational class when the U.S. census first listed it in 1870. Thirty years later, that number had increased to over ninety thousand. These commercial travelers made up a sizeable percentage of train passengers.

There's no doubt the smiling Harvey Girls, pleasant surroundings and delicious food helped lift the burden of the traveling salesmen's work; however, Fred Harvey went a step further. In the large Harvey hotels such as the Bisonte, there were designated Sample Rooms for salesmen to use to display their wares and meet potential customers. Winning the trust of locals was a challenge for the traveling businessmen, and many were eager to align themselves with the high regard and fine reputation of Fred Harvey.

According to an interview printed in a Santa Fe employee newsletter, the excitement of the trains arriving and departing at the Amarillo, Texas Santa Fe Depot first stirred Harvey Girl Opal Sells's imagination. The depot filled with train passengers several times a day, and she imagined the many places these travelers would visit. The challenge in front of her was learning the "Harvey Girl" way. The Harvey House manager, Mr. Lindsey, had been very kind; however, he made it clear that there were good reasons for the rules a Harvey Girl was required to follow. Some of the rules were not much different from what Momma had expected of Opal at home: be courteous and respectful; only speak when spoken to. However, remembering exactly how to place the knife and fork or from which side to serve the food to a customer wasn't as easy to remember. Fred Harvey's name was etched in the handle of the silverware and was a constant reminder of her employer's expectations.

Opal had grown up on a farm not far outside of town, and even in that rural setting, she had been expected to maintain a "proper" appearance. The Harvey rules that didn't allow makeup, required you to keep your hair neat and to always wear clean, crisply ironed dresses just came naturally. That's what Opal had always done. However, the table setting in the Texas farm kitchen that Opal and her mother shared was very simple compared to the Harvey House dining room. And their meals were certainly not as elaborate. Opal had never eaten, much less served, a five-course meal before.

The youngest of seven children, Opal had stayed home to care for her invalid mother. After her mother's death, the family was certain Opal, now in her mid-twenties, had missed her opportunity to find a husband. A charitable uncle paid her tuition to a business college, where she received secretarial training. However, it didn't take Opal long to realize that a career as a stenographer was not for her. "So I went in to see a manager at the Harvey House in Amarillo. He said to me, 'You're the first girl who has walked in here today who wasn't chewing gum. You look like our type.' He hired me that day, and I began work the next morning. I was real nervous." This possibility appealed to her sense of propriety, and she knew that if she worked hard she would have the opportunity to move to other Harvey Houses down the Santa Fe line.

Three years later, Opal Sells was leaving the familiar surroundings of the Texas Panhandle to work at the Bisonte, in Hutchinson, Kansas. She experienced the Hutchinson flood in 1929 and recalls that she and other Harvey Girls who lived in accommodations across the street from the hotel had to be carried by a male Harvey employee through the floodwaters to work. "We had to stay at the Bisonte for two or three days until the water subsided."

From Hutchinson, Opal was sent to the Union Terminal in Cleveland, Ohio, where she worked in the posh Fred Harvey restaurant, the English Oak

An unidentified man tries to catch fish in front of the Bisonte Harvey hotel, Hutchinson, Kansas, following a flood in the summer of 1929. *Courtesy of the Paul Everett Parker Jr. family.*

Harvey manager Paul Everett Parker Sr. with his wife, Grace, and son, Everett, at the Bisonte Harvey hotel, 1930, Hutchinson, Kansas. *Courtesy of the Paul Everett Parker Jr. family.*

Room. In 1933, Opal worked as a Harvey Girl in the Tea Room in the Straus Building at the Chicago World's Fair.

Years later, Opal settled in Albuquerque, New Mexico, and worked at the Alvarado Hotel there, ending her career with Fred Harvey as cashier in the Alvarado Coffee Shop. During a career with the Fred Harvey Company that spanned forty-five years, Opal worked in ten different Harvey establishments. While at the Alvarado, she married John S. Hill, who had been employed by the Santa Fe Railroad for the same number of years as Opal had been employed by Fred Harvey.

Paul Everett Parker joined the Fred Harvey management team in the mid-1920s. He had served in the U.S. Navy and studied restaurant management at Cornell University in Ithaca, New York, finishing there in 1918. Parker married Grace Carney Jackson on January 18, 1925, in Wichita, Kansas.

Paul and Grace met in Topeka, where she was attending finishing school and where he was most likely training and working in the Topeka Harvey House lunchroom. After their wedding, Paul was transferred to the Harvey House in Colorado Springs, Colorado. Their printed wedding announcement states, "At home after March first, Colorado Springs, Colo., Fred Harvey." The following year, Paul transferred to the Cardenas Harvey Hotel in Trinidad, Colorado. While there, the couple's son, Paul Jr., was born.

By 1929, Paul Sr. was managing the Bisonte in Hutchison. As best as the Parker family can determine, Grace Parker probably did not take on the

72

The Bisonte gardener, Mr. Smith, with Paul Everett Parker Jr., son of the Harvey manager, on the grounds of the Harvey hotel, Hutchinson, Kansas, 1930. *Courtesy of the Paul Everett Parker Jr. family.*

responsibilities of being chaperone and "house mother" to the Harvey Girls as many of the wives of Harvey managers did. She more likely focused on being a hostess to the Harvey House guests. Her husband is remembered for his attention to details and as having a somewhat formal attitude in his duties as manager of the large Kansas Harvey establishment. Parker kept notecards on frequent guests, recording information such as their favorite Harvey House meal or what, if anything, they added to their coffee. He might also add the names of children or other specific details that he could bring into the conversation during the guests' next visit to the Bisonte. Wearing a suit and tie and bestowing individual attention on each guest, Paul Everett Parker Sr. was surely a fine example of the Fred Harvey way of doing business.

In the summer of 1926, Fern Shoemaker Mohler needed a job to provide money for her return to McPherson College in McPherson, Kansas. She and some of her friends traveled thirty miles to Hutchinson to apply for waitressing jobs. These young women were simply looking for work. They were not looking for adventure or for husbands. Fern expressed in an article in a women's magazine in the early 1990s that it was much later that she realized that she had been a part of the Fred Harvey narrative. "It was the best kind of job for a girl to get for the summer. We all knew we had to work to get back to school the next year." None of the girls had waitressing experience, which ended up being a benefit. "They really preferred we not have experience so we could learn the way they did it."

Fern and her friends worked hard for a dollar a day, and had they not had the benefit of free room and board, the job would not have been financially advantageous. "We each had to keep the silver for the places we served polished, glasses shining and use only properly washed and mended linens." Fern's assignment was in the lunchroom of the Bisonte. "We also made sandwiches so they would be available to train passengers who were in a hurry or wanted something to eat later. Often we were so busy there was no time to get something for ourselves to eat." The college girls were expected to give quick, courteous service and serve the food in the Harvey way—always with a smile. "You had to work fast because the passengers would be in a hurry and they didn't want to wait," Fern said. "We worked eight hours a day six days a week, but many times the hours were in split shifts so more waitresses could be on duty during mealtimes. If we went to work or came home when it was dark, a Harvey bellhop escorted us. Our off-duty hours were spent in a dormitory in back of the hotel where a matron supervised our activities, and if we did go out, she made sure we were in before lights out." Fern remembers the rule prohibiting Harvey Girls from dating Harvey employees or railroad men. "That was strictly forbidden, but isn't it funny how many girls ended up marrying railroaders or bellhops?"

"The big excitement of each day was when the head red cap [bellhop] rang the brass gong and called: 'Train time.' The train conductor would take a head count of those who wanted to dine at the restaurant. He'd telegraph ahead the time of arrival and number of customers. We were always ready."

She worked as a Harvey Girl at the Bisonte for two summers, 1926 and 1928. After completing her degree at McPherson College, Fern taught school for several years, married a McPherson College professor and lived the rest of her life in McPherson. "For so many years I didn't think much about my summer job as a Harvey Girl," Fern said. "Waitresses were not very high on the social scale. For me to receive attention because of my summer job as a waitress seems very funny to me, but it is nice to be remembered." Fern participated in a panel discussion in Hutchinson in 1982 and, referring to the starched Harvey Girl uniforms, remarked, "Fellas used to say hugging a Harvey Girl was like trying to put your arm around a porcupine."

Harvey Girls pose beside their service areas in the dining room of the Bisonte, Hutchinson, Kansas. Many photos such as this were taken by the Fred Harvey Company staff photographer, Gay M. Hamilton. *Courtesy of Michael McMillan.*

Gertrude "Trudy" Hammond began her Harvey Girl career in Hutchinson, Kansas, in 1939. "I was trained by a head waitress at the lunch counter and started out only serving the train men. After two weeks of training, I was put in the dining room, where it was very formal with silver service and white tablecloths. Every day after the meals, we polished our glass goblets and silverware." Trudy worked a split shift: 6:30 a.m. to 9:00 a.m.; 11:00 a.m. to 2:00 p.m.; and 6:00 p.m. to 9:00 p.m. "We had to do our own bussing—food in and dirty dishes out." Her salary was twenty-five dollars a month with room and board and tips. "If we got a quarter or half-dollar tip, we were thrilled. We had a 9:00 p.m. curfew, and when we came in we had to sign the register at the front desk of the hotel. The help was not to go out with each other." This rule was often ignored by Harvey employees but not by Bisonte management. "I dated a bellhop and someone must have seen us," Trudy explained. "I was called in to the manager's office and fired." Soon after this, Trudy married the bellhop, Tom Ketring, and they moved to Newton, Kansas.

Harvey employees couldn't date, but it seems that getting married was allowed. "They hired me back in Newton," Trudy said. "During the next few years, we worked together—Tom as assistant manager and me as a Harvey Girl—in Dodge City, Kansas; Albuquerque, New Mexico; Gallup,

This trackside view of the Santa Fe Depot in Hutchinson, Kansas, shows the large corner Harvey newsstand. This convenient location attracted train passengers, who could purchase items such as newspapers, books, cigars and fresh fruit. *Courtesy of Michael McMillan.*

New Mexico, for the Indian Ceremonial; Winslow, Arizona; and Barstow, California. They moved us around a lot, and we didn't stay long at any one place."

In Barstow, the troop trains had begun moving World War II soldiers, and Japanese Americans were being sent by train to internment camps. Trudy remembers that the quality of the food was not always up to Harvey standards, but "we did the best we could. We made hundreds of sandwiches every day." Troop train and meal schedules were unpredictable, presenting a frustrating challenge to a Harvey staff accustomed to order and high standards.

Trudy related a situation in the Barstow kitchen while the staff was serving a troop train:

> *I had the officers so I had to clear, set up and serve first. My table had finished, and I was ready to serve the next group. I went into the kitchen for my servings. The plates were stacked on top of a steam table ready for the food. For some reason the chef refused to give me the food. Words were exchanged, and I snapped and started throwing those heavy plates at the chef. He picked up a meat clever and started around the steam table towards me but stopped suddenly. Our black salad boy, Arthur, was standing behind me with a large knife. He said, 'Don't*

you dare touch Miss Trudy!' Things calmed down a little, and I was able to finishing serving the meal. Later I was called into the manager's office and asked if I didn't think I owed the chef an apology. I said, 'no' and refused to do so. I wasn't fired, as my husband was the assistant manager.

When she was seventeen, in 1921, Josephine Klenke went to work at the Bisonte Hotel. She remembers the strict standards included the requirement that tablecloth creases had to be a certain way, toward the door. "If there was the least spot we had to change it and take it to the housekeeper to be washed. They each cost twenty-five dollars, and that was a lot of money back then." Over sixty years after her Harvey Girl days, Josephine is Sister Valeria, a retired nun. She summed up her Harvey career as one of "style, class and discipline."

The *Hutchinson News* printed a poignant farewell to the Bisonte in June 1946, when the hotel closed. The building was demolished approximately twenty years later.

Many a cold winter night, travelers warmed themselves by the great logs, flame-licked and throwing out heat and cheer from the mammoth fireplace. Many an elaborate dinner, prepared with an artist's touch by the chef over-lords of the red-tiled kitchen, was served by attractive Harvey Girls in the paneled dining room, a place of parade for Hutchinson society.

But an era in the city's history has now flickered out. The Bisonte, once the finest hotel in Kansas, has closed its doors to the general public, nominally at least, and become headquarters for the American Legion. Thus ends the period that saw transition from rude frontier days to the polish and culture of an easier life.

Longtime employees were recognized by the newspaper: Bill Braggs worked as a porter at the Bisonte for over thirty years. Joe Garcia, chef, and Mayme McGuire, newsstand manager, each had continuous employment for thirty-six years.

LAKIN

Guy Potter was the first manager in Fred Harvey's lunchroom in Topeka, but during the first year of operation (1876), he moved two hundred miles west to transform an existing Lakin hotel into a Harvey hotel, second in the quickly expanding Harvey chain. A small Santa Fe Depot sat east of the newly established Harvey House. Accounts of Potter's responsibilities in establishing the Lakin site vary. The *History of Kearny County, Kansas*, Vol. 1, states, "Guy Potter, uncle of D.H. Browne, established an eating house at Lakin in April 1875 to accommodate the passengers and train crews passing from Dodge City to Granada, Co. This was taken over and enlarged by Fred Harvey in 1877 and was the center of the railroad activities and social life of the town until it was moved to Coolidge in December 1880."

Other accounts have Fred Harvey and Guy Potter working together in other business endeavors prior to the opening of the Topeka lunchroom. This, in my opinion, makes it unlikely that Potter would have established a business competing with Harvey's; however, almost 140 years later, it is very difficult to learn the true details of the business relationship between these two men. We do know for certain that for a few years there was a Harvey House in Lakin.

The 1880 census listed the following Harvey House employees, including two members of the Harvey family: Matthew Fisher, manager; Frank Fisher, clerk; Florence Beauman, niece of Fred Harvey, waitress; Charles Beauman, nephew of Fred Harvey, clerk; Samuel L. Phillips, chef; Carrie E. Phillips, Mary Welch and Louisa Dickhil, waitresses; Freddy Bettrdy, cook; Fredericka Dunkard, dishwasher; William Jacobis, servant; and Kitty Filbourne, chambermaid.

This specific information about the Lakin staff confirms that in some, if not all, early Harvey locations women were hired as waitresses. This would be prior to the event in Raton, New Mexico, in 1882 that is usually credited for the idea of hiring young women instead of men to staff Harvey Houses.

Approximately three years after the Harvey House was established in Lakin, the building was dismantled and moved to a site at that time called Sargent, two miles from the Colorado-Kansas state line. Four years later, a Santa Fe division point was established just west of Sargent in Coolidge, leaving Sargent virtually deserted and Coolidge flourishing.

Roaming buffalo herds impeded train travel in remote Kansas sites such as Lakin, occasionally delaying forward movement. Harvey manager Potter reported waiting aboard a train for almost two hours while the large prairie beasts crossed the track. During the delay, the brakeman positioned in the caboose shot thirteen buffalo.

There is no doubt that at one time, for perhaps a very short period, Lakin thrived. Fourth of July festivities there in 1879 were hosted by Fred and Sally

Harvey. Their guests included wealthy Kansas rancher Colonel Richard Hardesty, along with many other influential businessmen, politicians and ranchers. The entire Harvey family attended, along with Mrs. Harvey's young, single sister, Margaret "Maggie" Mattas. Colonel Hardesty, still unmarried at age forty-six, was considered one of the most eligible bachelors in the West. It isn't difficult to imagine what happened at the party. The couple danced many dances that night, and early the next year, the two were married at the Harveys' home in Leavenworth, Kansas.

A drawing of Lakin during the time the Harvey House was thriving provided by the Kearny County Historical Society shows little more than a dozen buildings on one side of the railroad tracks and three small buildings on the opposite side. Beyond this you see nothing but Kansas prairie. In these early, remote Kansas settlements, Harvey Houses were established as much, if not more so, to serve the railroad employees as well as train passengers. Therefore, in these early years of the railroad's development, as division points were established and moved, the number of railroad personnel fluctuated, sometimes eliminating the need for a restaurant or hotel.

It would be interesting to know whether the strict Fred Harvey rules of service were observed in these frontier Harvey Houses. Were less experienced Harvey Girls sent to towns such as Lakin and Coolidge where fewer train passengers crowded the restaurant several times a day? Or perhaps a woman with more experience would request these desolate locations, realizing her workdays would probably be less demanding even if marriage prospects were diminished.

Carrie E. Phillips Davies, a waitress and housekeeper at the Lakin Harvey House, explained that train service in 1878 was "very limited, since we had but two trains a day, one from the east and one from the west." Mrs. Davies observed antelope in great herds, as well as buffalo and wild horses passing the hotel on their way to the nearby Arkansas River for water. "One of my first experiences after coming to the Harvey House was to serve a party of Indians and their interpreter. The Ute Indians had gone on the war path and had killed the Indian agent, so government authorities took thirty of them to Washington, and they stopped at our eating house on their way."

Carrie was instrumental in starting a stand of trees in 1879 shortly after moving to Lakin. "I had been raised in the beautiful Shenandoah Valley of Virginia and the western country [of Kansas] looked very cold and barren to me since there were no trees of any kind to be seen far or near except along the river. I decided it was because people were negligent in planting and caring for things that there was such a shortage and that I was going

This preserved tree trunk is displayed in the Kearny County Museum as a tribute to a stand of trees that once grew in front of the Lakin Harvey House. Harvey Girl Carey Phillip Davies missed the lush trees of her native Virginia and ordered a dozen trees from Florence, Kansas, to plant in her yard. She soon discovered the ground was too hard to plant the trees and that she did not have ready access to water to keep them alive. The manager of the Harvey House purchased the elm and cottonwood trees from Carrie and planted them. For quite some time, these were the only thriving trees in Lakin. *Courtesy of Kearny County Historical Society.*

to be [a woman] who would have an eastern home in a western state." She ordered one and a half dozen trees from Florence, Kansas, at a total cost of $3.50. "Part were elm and part were cottonwood. Of course I was elated over the prospect of a beautiful home with a lovely shady yard." When the trees arrived, the ground was so hard that Carrie found it impossible to dig holes to plant. "Mr. Fisher, manager of the hotel, bought them off me and planted them in the front yard [of the Harvey House] where there was water available." The trees were a novelty, and "all the Harvey House and railroad employees became interested in their care—even the trainmen who stopped for meals."

Carrie's trees stood in Lakin far longer than the Harvey House existed; however, this remote site holds a place in Fred Harvey history as the second of many successful Harvey hotels.

NEWTON

Newton's early history includes some very wild, unsettled times. In the late 1870s, the town was known as "Bloody Newton, the wickedest town in the West" because of the large number of deaths within its boundaries. Many cowboys stopped here and received their pay following a long, dusty, lonely trail ride, and there was little that could be done to contain their reckless behavior.

After a decade of trying to cope with these negative elements, the cattle business had moved to Dodge City, and Newton began to clean up its town and its reputation. The new Newton slogan was "Now Notice Newton!"

Certainly, the building of the Fred Harvey Arcade Hotel in 1900 was a pivotal event in Newton's transformation. A few years later, the Harvey

Three-story Harvey hotel, the Arcade, Newton, Kansas. *Courtesy of Michael McMillan.*

Left: The label on the milk can identifies this as a Fred Harvey product. Ahead of its time, the Fred Harvey Company was establishing its brand over a century before "branding" became a buzzword. *Photo by Beau Gentry. Courtesy of Skip Gentry's Fred Harvey Memorabilia Collection.*

Right: The Harvey ranch, dairy and creamery, located approximately two miles outside of Newton, Kansas, provided products to Harvey Houses along the line. Harvey used the railroad to ship supplies, food and employees throughout the Harvey system and wasn't required to pay for these services. *Photo by Beau Gentry. Courtesy of Skip Gentry's Fred Harvey Memorabilia Collection.*

district headquarters was relocated from Kansas City, Missouri, making Newton the operating headquarters for more than half of the Harvey eating system.

Newton became home to a Harvey dairy, meat locker storage, a creamery, an ice plant, a poultry feeding station and a modern steam laundry. A carbonating plant for bottling soda pop was established, and root beer, ginger ale, cola and club soda produced in Newton filled bottles with "Fred Harvey—Newton" stamped on the bottom. These soft drinks were sold exclusively in Fred Harvey dining facilities, newsstands and on Santa Fe passenger cars. In 1914, Coca-Cola issued a franchise to the Fred Harvey company to bottle its product at the Newton facility.

This battered wooden shipping crate traveled many railroad miles. Fred Harvey used thousands of containers such as this to deliver hotel and restaurant supplies via the Santa Fe at no charge. *Photo by Beau Gentry. Courtesy of Skip Gentry's Fred Harvey Memorabilia Collection.*

Wooden shipping crates with sections might have been used to ship private-label Fred Harvey whiskey. Most shipping containers that have survived are stamped with the Fred Harvey name and "Newton, Kansas," which was a center for producing and shipping Harvey products. *Photo by Beau Gentry. Courtesy of Skip Gentry's Fred Harvey Memorabilia Collection.*

The Newton Harvey general store was remodeled in 1910 at an estimated cost of $10,000. Combined, the entire Newton Harvey operation employed hundreds and helped alter the town's rowdy reputation. Supplies for Harvey Houses and newsstands were shipped to Newton and then distributed down the line. Picture postcards, magazines and other merchandise for all Harvey newsstands first came to Newton. Trains brought carloads of corn, peas and other canned goods to Newton, where these items were stored and parceled out to other Harvey House locations. Fresh fruits and vegetables were handled the same way but shipped much more frequently.

The August 31, 1911 edition of the *Newton Evening Kansan-Republican* included an extensive review of the Arcade as part of a story chronicling the positive changes that had come about in Newton:

> *Alongside the depot is the Fred Harvey hotel known as the Arcade, where Manager Maguire conducts a most homelike hostelry. Though this house is by no means the most pretentious on the system, he and his able assistants have made quite a reputation for the Arcade. Last month health inspectors for the state dropped off at Newton, and according to the* Kansas-Republican, *this is how they found things under Mr. Maguire's management.*
>
> *The Arcade was found to be in perfect condition in every way. Manager Maguire is to be congratulated on the excellent condition of everything in his hotel. As the inspectors passed from room to room they would pass their hands across the top of a door or the back of a mirror or along the wall, but their hands remained clean, for there was no dust. Even a whack on the carpet or on a mattress brought forth no dust. All this shows the efficient work that is going on at the Arcade and the care taken for the comfort and health of the traveler.*

Attention to detail was always the hallmark of a Fred Harvey establishment. Fresh flowers were on display regardless of how remote the location. When the Kansas state flower was in bloom, the Arcade lobby and dining room were decorated with sunflowers, and the hotel manager usually sported a large bloom in his lapel.

Ongoing maintenance of buildings and furnishings was also a priority. Seven years after the Arcade opened, all of the furniture was revarnished and the seats of all chairs replaced. The Harvey company employed men who specialized in upholstering and finishing furniture and sent them to Harvey Houses to work. The men were expected to work at the Arcade for at least two months retouching every piece of furniture.

The Newton Harvey House staff, taken in the 1940s. The five women kneeling in front were newsstand employees. *Courtesy of Helen Collins.*

There are many stories and records indicating the large number of World War II troops traveling by train who were fed in Harvey Houses, but little has been said about the First World War. A news story that appeared on October 6, 1917, reported that the restaurant in the Arcade served dinner to 645 soldiers in an hour and twenty minutes. "Harvey manager, Milton Browne, and his force of employes [*sic*] set a record when the train of drafted men of Arizona and New Mexico stopped in Newton. The number seated at each time was 272. Extra chairs were used at all the tables in the dining room and the lobby was cleared of all its furniture and long tables arranged for accommodation of about one hundred. This work was accomplished with little extra help although members of the St. Cecilia guild poured drinks."

Newton was a very energetic railroad town, and even in peacetime, Harvey Girls were often faced with multiple trains, with many passengers arriving at mealtime. One reporter described the first "supper" train arriving at 5:50 p.m., and between that time and 8:00 p.m., seven trains stopped for supper in the dining room at the Arcade. Sixty-five passengers from one train dined at the restaurant, and other trains averaged fifty.

Some elements of the Newton community were slow to adapt to the new Newton. The Harvey management was having trouble with "loafers" who were hanging out in front of the hotel. It seems that the rock used to decorate the exterior base of the building provided a comfortable spot for men to lounge and watch those coming and going at the Arcade. That alone might not have been a problem, but the men used tobacco, and there was no place to spit but on the sidewalk. Decorative boards were added to the building façade making it impossible to sit or lean on the rock. Without comfortable seating, the men moved on, and the Arcade regained its dignity.

Approximately two miles out of Newton, Harvey established a five-hundred-acre farm operation with 150 employees, where cattle, poultry and produce for the restaurants were raised. The Harvey dairy and creamery was also located here. The Newton newspaper proclaimed this location to be a very smart decision by the Harvey company: "Most any form of animal or vegetable life thrives in Kansas, and no one spot to greater advantage than around Newton." The farm continued to be productive until 1960, when the operation was shut down.

Beginning her Harvey Girl career in Amarillo, Texas, in 1929, Desree Arrowood also worked in the Waynoka, Oklahoma Harvey House for a short period and was then transferred to Emporia and Dodge City. "Then I was lucky enough to be chosen to go to Newton when the new house opened there. It was exciting. Times were hard, and I felt I was very lucky in

Fred Harvey Dairy Farm, Newton, Kansas. *Courtesy of Helen Collins.*

Dairy cows at the Harvey farm just outside Newton, Kansas. Fred Harvey publicity photos were not limited to Harvey employees. *Courtesy of Helen Collins.*

more than one way. We had a nice place to live, a good house mother and good managers." Desree left her Harvey House employ when she married in 1933. The newlyweds traveled by train to honeymoon at the Chicago World's Fair.

Amelia Raesler was born in the Prussian part of Germany in 1871 and immigrated with her family to the United States in 1880. Within a year of arriving in this country, Amelia's mother died in childbirth. Soon after this tragic event, her father went to Chicago to look for work and was never heard from again. Amelia, her four sisters and one brother were adopted by different families. Amelia's adopted family eventually settled in Newton, Kansas. When she turned eighteen, Amelia went to work at the local Harvey House, and from there she worked her way west. After three years as a Harvey Girl in Newton, Syracuse and Dodge City, Kansas, and La Junta, Colorado, a co-worker told her about a mountain of silver that had been discovered at Creede, Colorado. Adventuresome Amelia quit her job to go find that mountain. In Creede, there was no Harvey House, but she found work nursing a young man who had been thrown from his horse and suffered a concussion. Once he recovered from his injuries, the couple married. Amelia and Frank bought land and developed a large ranch extending over six thousand acres in Colorado.

In 1930, the Harvey House lunchroom, dining room and employee living quarters were moved to the depot, and the Arcade Hotel was demolished. With the onset of the Depression and changes in the demands for railroad service, railroad offices and headquarters were moved from Newton to Albuquerque.

A telephone interview with former Harvey Girl Helen Boese Collins provided insight into the Harvey House operations of the early 1950s. Soon after she married in September 1953, Helen was hired at the Newton Harvey House and continued there until the restaurant closed on May 5, 1957. She was paid forty-five cents an hour and scheduled to work eight hours a day, five or six days a week. "There were times I pulled double shifts on the [lunch] counter," Helen said. "I was supposed to work 3:00 p.m. to 11:00 p.m., but some days I worked 3:00 to 7:00 the next morning because some of the 11:00 shift were 'no shows.'" The waitresses were given their work schedule each week, but they were always considered "on call" to come to work and were not paid overtime. "By this time, there were many dining cars, and passengers didn't have to come into a Harvey House to eat. The majority of my customers were local or were at the depot to catch a train."

An unidentified hostess in the Harvey House dining room, Newton, Kansas, mid-1950s. *Courtesy of the Harvey County Historical Society.*

Mr. and Mrs. Leland Moore are seated in the Harvey House lunchroom, Newton, Kansas. An example of the changes in Harvey standards during the last few years of operation is the absence of the trademark linen tablecloths on the dining tables in the background. *Courtesy of the Harvey County Historical Society.*

Helen was sent to Gallup, New Mexico, to work for a week during the Indian Centennial. Her experiences there were quite different than in Kansas. "Looking out the back door of the Harvey House all you could see on the hillside were teepees and Indians. We wore bright-colored Mexican-style skirts and a blouse with ruffles. But the rules were still the rules."

After Helen returned to Newton, she was moved to the dining room, where tips were better. "It was a good job, especially for a woman. You got to keep your own tips. In other restaurants, your tips were put into a jar and split at the end of the day." Most of the Harvey employees at this time were Newton residents. "Only one Harvey Girl lived in the dorms upstairs because she was single. The manager lived in an apartment upstairs but wasn't required to live on the premises."

The current Amtrak station in Newton, designed by Kansas architect E.H. Harrison, was built in 1929–30 in the Tudor Revival style and was modeled after Shakespeare's house in Stratford-upon-Avon. This two-story brick building was constructed with a steep slate roof and patches of half-timbering. The interior has some remaining medieval touches of heavy-beamed ceilings and half-timbered walls.

This building is the third depot at this location. In its heyday, it housed a ticket office, a waiting room, railroad offices, a Harvey House dining room and a lunchroom with two counters. The Arcade Hotel, a Harvey House hotel, opened in 1900, replacing an earlier structure from 1883. Today, the depot building houses the Amtrak waiting room and provides space for a variety of shops and offices, including a law office that takes up the space once occupied by the Harvey House lunchroom and newsstand.

The station was added to both the National Register of Historic Places and the Kansas Register of Historic Places in 1985 and is part of the Newton Main Street Historical District II, as designated in 2003.

SYRACUSE

Syracuse is in far western Kansas approximately sixteen miles from the Colorado state line. The town, founded in 1873, was originally named Holidaysburg. In 1878, it was renamed Syracuse after the city in New York.

A promotional guide for train passengers distributed by the Santa Fe Railroad included the following, somewhat effusive, description of Fred

The Sequoyah Hotel, Syracuse, Kansas. *Courtesy of Michael McMillan.*

The large, beautifully decorated dining room of the Sequoyah Hotel, Syracuse, Kansas. *Courtesy of Michael McMillan.*

Harvey service: "At Fred Harvey's you are always expected. The girls are ever in their best bib and tucker, spotlessly gowned, manicured, groomed, combed, dental-flossed—bright, healthy intelligent girls—girls that are never fly, flip or fresh, but who give you the attention that never obtrudes, but which is hearty and heartfelt." The marketing copywriters were in high gear when they wrote this.

The wooden, two-story building that was originally the Lakin Harvey House and then dismantled and moved to Coolidge eventually ended up in Syracuse around 1888. The building was destroyed by fire.

The expansive Sequoyah Harvey Hotel, a favorite of Harvey Girls, was designed by Louis Curtiss and replaced the earlier Harvey House. Originally the Grand Hotel, the building was acquired by the Fred Harvey Company and thoroughly overhauled following Curtiss's design at a reported cost of $100,000. The Sequoyah opened in July 1908 with fifteen guest rooms, a lunchroom that seated 51 and a dining room that served 110.

As beautiful as the Sequoyah was with wide arches and a beautiful patio adjacent to the dining room, the grounds surrounding this western Kansas Harvey House were even more impressive. Train passengers were greeted with a plush lawn that covered almost two blocks and was decorated with large beds of flowers.

Earl Augustus Reynolds began his career with Fred Harvey at age sixteen as a dishwasher at the Sequoya. In less than two years, he had worked his way up to the position of chef. He was transferred to the Harvey House in Belen, New Mexico, and after serving in the military during World War I, he was chef at Gran Quivira, the Harvey hotel in Clovis, New Mexico. Upon his retirement after working for the Fred Harvey Company for twenty years, Earl Augustus Reynolds was described as a quiet, soft-spoken man who was "terribly in love with his work."

Joanne Stinelichner was hired as a Harvey Girl in 1916 at the age of twenty-two, soon after arriving in the United States from Germany. She lived with an aunt in Wisconsin and after she had begun to learn English, she and two friends went to Chicago to interview to become Harvey Girls. All three were hired, and Joanne was sent to Hutchinson, Kansas, where she stayed for two years. She had never been in a Harvey House, but she adjusted quickly and enjoyed her job and the people she met. "The manager in Hutchinson was Irish, and he liked me right away."

After transferring to Syracuse, Joanne began secretly dating the chef, John Thompson. A friendly night watchman assisted in the clandestine romance by helping Joanne get back into the Harvey House after curfew.

Sixteen-year-old Earl A. Reynolds (second from right) with the chef and kitchen staff at the Sequoyah in Syracuse, Kansas. *Courtesy of Louise Reynolds and family.*

Three Harvey Girls along with part of the Sequoyah staff, Syracuse, Kansas, in the early 1900s. *Courtesy of Louise Reynolds and family.*

Perhaps the relationship wasn't much of a secret after all—later, the couple was married in the manager's apartment. Both continued to work and were given a room together in the Harvey employee living quarters. A few years later, Joanne and John were working in Emporia, Kansas, when their daughter, Helen, was born. "I worked up to the end of the ninth month. I was on my shift in Emporia when my water broke!" The husband and wife were valued, longtime employees, and after John's death in 1927, arrangements were made for a Harvey maid or waitresses to look after their four-year-old daughter upstairs while Joanne worked her shift in the Harvey restaurant downstairs.

Joanne loved her many years working for Fred Harvey and after retirement gave many interviews about her experiences. She recalled the family atmosphere: "The girls were like my family, my daughters." She remembers that "Harvey Girls were very happy women." Joanne worked for Fred Harvey until 1948 managing Harvey establishments from Kansas to California.

The beautiful, elegant Sequoyah closed in 1936, and the building was later demolished.

WELLINGTON

Wellington was a division point on the Santa Fe Railroad and was headquarters for the part of the Santa Fe line in Kansas known as the Panhandle Division. Wellington had a Santa Fe office building, as well as a roundhouse, a depot and a Harvey House for travelers. Wellington's original Harvey House restaurant opened in 1881 and was replaced in 1907 with a large stone building. According to Fred Harvey Company records, the new Wellington Harvey House dining room seated seventy-two, the lunchroom seated sixty-seven and there were nineteen guest rooms, although newspaper reports at the time stated there were ten guest rooms. A kitchen, bakery, walk-in refrigerator and storeroom were also built into the structure. A sophisticated "egg boiler" was included in the kitchen. The breakfast cook would dial the length of time he wanted eggs to cook, and when eggs placed in a basket were lowered into the boiling water, the timer automatically started. The instant the time was up, the egg basket raised out of the water, and the boiled eggs were ready to serve.

The Wellington newspaper ran a lengthy article explaining how the high standards were maintained throughout the Harvey eating house system. "The Fred Harvey superintendent or the assistant is likely to drop in at any time. When he comes, he goes thru [*sic*] several of the rooms, and with a silk handkerchief wipes over the tops of the doors and other unseen and outoftheway [*sic*] places. On his handkerchief is the least particle soiled after the test, somebody has to explain. He then tries several of the carpets, which he scrapes with the sole of his shoe, and if a particle of dust settles on his shiny patent leather, the manager is called 'onto the carpet.'" I can only imagine the difficulty of maintaining such cleanliness at all times in wind-swept Kansas.

Built of Nostic stone, this Santa Fe Depot and Harvey House was also designed by Kansas architect Louis Curtiss and cost approximately $45,000. The building was a long horizontal building typical of rail stations being constructed at the time; however, the stone exterior and elements of Dutch Colonial and Spanish Colonial/Mission designs gave this Harvey House a distinctive look. It took five boxcars of furniture to furnish the Wellington Harvey House, and every guest room had hot and cold running water and telephone service. However, Harvey hotel accommodations in Wellington were small compared to other Kansas Harvey hotels because the town already had a hotel that was owned by local merchants. Traveling salesmen, who made up a large percentage of train travelers and hotel guests, were loyal to that hotel, as it was owned by their local customers. This situation

Designed by architect Louis Curtiss, this Harvey hotel in Wellington, Kansas, had a dining room that seated seventy-two, a lunchroom that served sixty-seven and nineteen guest rooms. *Courtesy of Michael McMillan.*

was newsworthy, as the *Evening Kansan-Republican* in Newton reported, "It is said that a commercial man going to Wellington to sell his goods must not stay any place but at the hotel owned by the local business men, that is, if he wishes to meet with success in that town."

Louis DeBold was the first manager of the new Wellington Harvey House, and the first meals were served in the restaurant on November 1, 1907. Typical of the Harvey organization, the manager's wife was placed in charge of the second floor, where the Harvey Girls lived. Twenty Harvey employees opened the new establishment: a cashier, a chef, a second cook, a headwaiter, a baker, waitresses and chamber maids.

In 1910, Charlotta Ward was the manager of the Wellington Harvey House and at the time was the only female manager in the Harvey system, although in later years several Harvey Girls were promoted to manager. Mrs. Ward's husband was a Harvey manager, and after he became very ill, she took over most of his responsibilities and became the "unofficial" manager. After Mr. Ward's death, she convinced Harvey executives in Kansas City to give her a permanent job as manager.

The Wellington Harvey House manager prior to Mrs. Ward was Fred Kihm. He was drawn completely out of the realm of his normal responsibilities when he rescued a man twice within a few minutes from

Harvey House staff in the 1920s, Wellington, Kansas. *Courtesy of kansasmemory.org, Kansas State Historical Society.*

being crushed under the wheels of a passenger train. The incident was reported in the *Santa Fe* magazine:

> *The stranger made a dash for No. 14 with a suitcase in one hand. He caught the handrail but missed the step and swung against the journal box. Then he swung out over the platform and back over the rail. Mr. Kihm ran up and grabbed him, pulling him away from the rail. But instead of releasing his hold on the proper moment he hung onto the handrail and swung back over the track. Losing his hold, he fell over the rail. Instantly Kihm grabbed him again and pulled him away before the rear trucks reached him. The man, still grasping the suitcase, picked himself up and darted after the rear end of the train, which he caught. The passenger did not take time to thank Mr. Kihm or to bid him good-by.*

In every town where there was a Harvey House, local folks took advantage of the good food served in stylish surroundings. Local organizations had their banquets and annual meetings at the Harvey House, and the younger generations often made the restaurant a late night stop after an evening out on the town. It was reported in a column called "Mostly for Women Folks" in *The Wellington Daily News* that in December "Foss Farrar will be over from Arkansas City to attend the Polka Dot-Bob Cat party at the Harvey House." Oh, how I wish we had pictures of this event!

Train platforms were designed to provide a safe walking surface between the train and depot in most Kansas towns. Along the Santa Fe line, the bricks for these platforms were often supplied by the brick manufacturer in Coffeyville, Kansas. Large deposits of shale, limestone and building stone, in addition to an abundance of natural resources, provided the perfect location for a number of brick plants at the turn of the twentieth century. Bricks were also manufactured in Ottawa, and the Ottawa depot contains bricks from Coffeyville, Humboldt and Ottawa.

Coffeyville used a hard-firing process and local clay to produce bricks that could withstand the "freeze-and-thaw" cycle of harsh winter weather. At the turn of the nineteenth century, this was one of the largest brick manufacturers in the country. At their peak, the plants produced over 750,000 bricks daily that would eventually find their way to the streets and sidewalks of developing towns as well as train platforms.

The Wellington Harvey House closed in 1939, and the depot and Harvey House building was demolished in 1965.

5

TRACKSIDE RESTAURANTS

Good Eats

Arkansas City

Arkansas City was established in 1870 as Walnut City at the confluence of the Arkansas and Walnut Rivers, just a few miles north of the Oklahoma state line. Two years later, the name was changed to Arkansas City and is often referred to as "Ark City." After the railroad began its aggressive development at the turn of the century, the town had an elegant opera house and several fine hotels. Between 1889 and 1893, when settlers were swarming to claim newly opened land in the Indian Territory, many congregated in Ark City, and some reports say the town population grew to well over 100,000. After the rush, the town maintained its previous population of 5,000. (An unrelated author's note: both parents of actress Elizabeth Taylor were born in Arkansas City, and it is reported that she occasionally visited the town.)

The founders of Arkansas City spent almost ten years trying to bring railroad service to their town, including giving land worth $50,000 to the ATSF for the train right of way. When the first passenger train pulled into town in 1880, the depot, telegraph office, baggage and mail offices were in a wooden-frame building. The town had raised an additional $10,000 to build a depot and contributed fifty acres of land to build the railroad shops. A year later, the Santa Fe made Arkansas City a divisional point.

Some accounts show that the Arkansas City Harvey House opened in 1883; however, architectural plans show that construction of the structure

Arkansas City, Kansas Harvey House and Santa Fe Depot. *Courtesy of Michael McMillan.*

that housed the depot and Harvey House began in 1887. Caroline H. Applegate reported about the development of the railroad in Arkansas City for the town's bicentennial celebration in 1980. She recalls that the depot and railroad shops were completed by 1888 and that the Harvey House opened approximately three years later. While I cannot account for this particular variation in information, I know that in some situations when the Harvey House and train depot occupied the same building, records show the same opening date for the depot and Harvey House. In reality, completion of the interior of the Harvey House, including installation of kitchen equipment, might take longer, delaying the date when food service actually began. It *is* clearly documented that the Harvey House closed on June 1, 1933. The dining room was used during World War II as a canteen for the Red Cross to serve the soldiers on troop trains that passed through Arkansas City.

The expansive red brick Colonial-style depot building was trimmed in white stone and had a dark green roof. A large copper weather vane in the shape of a miniature locomotive sat atop a large dome in the center of the building. Fabricated by the Beard Foundry in Arkansas City, the weather vane became a well-known landmark. Large, arched windows stretched across the entire track side of the building, shaded by a corrugated iron awning. At one end of the building, a small park was installed. According to a news story in July 1888, the basement of the building contained storerooms, closets and a laundry facility. "In the laundry is the latest improved Hawley dryer. The head for the apparatus is furnished from a patent stove, jacketed with mineral wool, which prevents any heat from escaping into the laundry." The Harvey House kitchen, on ground level, was "large and airy" and contained storerooms, a pastry room, a silver and glassware room and a cold-air refrigerator. In what we've grown to recognize as typical Harvey style, the large dining room was stately and particularly impressive for Kansas at the end of the nineteenth century. The room had two walls of windows and an elegant red oak mantle fireplace with a "tile face, colonial style andirons and fire box." An imposing stained-glass window was installed above the fireplace. The newswriter describes the lunchroom as "fitted up in elegant style and containing all the modern conveniences known to man." (While not specifically descriptive, this style of "over the top" writing was prevalent in the late nineteenth and early twentieth centuries.) The building was lighted by a combination of gas and electric fixtures called "combination electroliers."

The Ark City depot had a second story containing nine "well furnished, large, airy sleeping apartments provided with all necessary closets." These apartments were the Harvey Girl accommodations.

The contractor for the building of the depot and Harvey House, Mr. Crilly, described the building in the news story: "The workmanship is superior, the style of architecture is grander and it is the most complete depot and eating house in the west." The Ark City Harvey dining room seated eighty-eight and the lunchroom thirteen.

One often-repeated story of the Kansas Harvey House lore is that an English nobleman, when he returned home after a tour of the United States, was asked about his most pleasant experience during his trip. He supposedly answered, "Breakfast at the Harvey House in Arkansas, Kansas."

Most likely, the nobleman was served his delicious breakfast by a Harvey Girl who was a resident of Arkansas City. This Harvey House hired primarily local women who usually lived in the second-floor living quarters to ensure they were on hand to serve passengers regardless of when the trains arrived.

The partnership between Fred Harvey and the Santa Fe had many benefits, even on a local level. Instances were recorded when a train would pull past the Arkansas depot platform until the sleeper cars were almost in front of the Harvey House. This required passengers in the forward coaches to walk over rough terrain back to the depot. It was claimed that this was done to benefit the Harvey House and to prevent usually more affluent sleeper-car passengers from going to a nearby restaurant. Once the passengers had all left the train, it was backed up to facilitate the unloading of baggage, express and mail. Locals joked that it probably delayed the mail, but maybe the Harvey people needed the money.

The Fred Harvey rule that Harvey Girls could not be married was most likely not as ironclad as we might think. During my research and conversations with former Harvey employees, I've learned that enforcement of this rule varied depending on the Harvey House manager and the availability of qualified employees.

In Arkansas, Kansas, in 1903, it appears the edict was wavering or perhaps completely ignored by Harvey manager Starkweather. After two Harvey employees, Jeremiah Cook and Annette Wiskstrom, were married, Starkweather announced that "in view of the fact that this is the second wedding that has occurred among the people working for me, I want to announce for the benefit of whom it may concern, that I am not running a matrimonial agency."

A marriage announcement in the local newspaper described the groom, M.D. Blair, as a railway mail service clerk based in Newton, and the bride, Miss Lessie Sadler, as having been "in charge of the lunch counter at the Harvey eating house in Arkansas City for a number of years." The couple rode the train to their future home in Newton immediately after the ceremony, but the new Mrs. Blair would no longer work for Fred Harvey. We have no way of knowing if the new bride was forced to leave her Harvey employment because she married or because her new husband's income was sufficient for the couple.

In January 1902, the Pastime Club of Arkansas City held its annual ball and banquet at the Harvey House. According to an account of the evening in the *Arkansas City Daily Traveler*, after a grand march and dancing that continued until 11:30 p.m., attendees were driven to the Harvey eating house, where a sumptuous banquet was served. "Hidden behind a bank of potted plants, a mandolin club filled the air with strains of sweet music, which, coupled with the decorations made the scene a pleasing one." The menu, described as "probably the finest ever put out for a banquet in the city included: Bouillon, wine, blue point oysters with celery and olives, small patties of sweet breads a la Victoria, roast squab with fine herb dressing and potato croquettes." Following this course, champagne was served before roast tenderloin of beef, lobster salad and cold boiled ham were brought to the guests, accompanied by Vienna rolls and plain bread. Almond ice cream and assorted cakes were the dessert choices.

In the summer of 1902, a large group of Texas Shriners riding in six Pullman sleepers passed through Arkansas City en route to San Francisco for an annual meeting. The local newspaper reported that the group took breakfast in the Arkansas City Harvey House, where the Harvey staff served eighty-six meals. This service would have been in addition to the regular breakfast run for locals, railroad men and passengers riding regularly scheduled trains.

In the summer of 1904, a portion of the Santa Fe Depot over the waiting rooms was converted into a two-story building to provide living space for Harvey House employees. The space formerly used by the employees served as guest rooms, "making quite an improvement over the present arrangement," according to the *Arkansas City Daily Traveler*.

Top: This silver ice bucket is an example of the high-quality serving pieces used in Harvey House dining rooms. It is one of several thousand pieces assembled by the late Skip Gentry, who was clearly a frontrunner for having the largest collection of Fred Harvey memorabilia *ever*. Through the efforts of his children, Danyelle Gentry Peterson and Beau Gentry, Skip's enthusiasm and energy lives on through his collection. *Photo by Beau Gentry. Courtesy of Skip Gentry's Fred Harvey Memorabilia Collection.*

Right: This Kold Pak insulated container kept food fresh during shipping, making it possible for diners in Harvey restaurants across Kansas to enjoy menu items such as oysters and fresh trout. *Photo by Beau Gentry. Courtesy of Skip Gentry's Fred Harvey Memorabilia Collection.*

A picture postcard shows the plush garden area adjacent to the depot and Harvey House, Arkansas City, Kansas. *Courtesy of Michael McMillan.*

Within two years, business at the Ark City Harvey House required an addition to the original dining room, making room for a larger lunch counter. The original lunch counter became part of the men's waiting room. (This indicates that there were separate depot waiting areas for men and women.)

Regardless of the intention of Fred Harvey to present a flawless dining experience and accommodations for train passengers, the operation of Harvey Houses was not without its challenges. Daily newspaper stories about events at the Harvey House were common. The *Arkansas City Daily Traveler* provided details of club meetings and ladies' parties at the "Harvey eating house." With a daily paper to produce and a very different journalistic attitude than later evolved, residents of "Ark City" could depend on the *Traveler* in the early 1900s for news such as: "The colored man who pounds the Chinese warpan at the Harvey eating house, at train time, has his work down so pat that he rattles out ragtime."

The custom at Fred Harvey's "eating houses" was to use local products when available and when they met Harvey's high standards. Arkansas City Bottling Works used its association with the respected restaurants as part of its advertising: "Now Listen! The Fred Harvey eating houses on the Santa Fe system are using our bottled soda water this season. That means the goods are the best that can be made. These people won't handle anything but the very best. See what an advertisement that makes for the Arkansas City Bottling Works. When you are dry ask the man at the counter for a bottle of A.C. Soda. Don't take any other. If he doesn't sell it, go to a good place."

In the early years of the Ark City Harvey House, it was a common stop to feed prisoners who were being transported by train. One story related that six prisoners who were on their way to the Fort Leavenworth facility "took supper at the Harvey eating house and seemed to enjoy their last meal outside of prison. The federal prisoners are: Chas. Bazi, counterfeiting, 3 years; Frank Jones, counterfeiting, 2 years; Henry Hartman 5 years, Max Dox 3 years and Bob Avery 3 years, for post-office robbery; Clay Axhelm attempted murder, 10 years." These uncharacteristic Harvey House customers were accompanied by deputy United States marshal Hale. On another occasion, thirty prisoners on their way to the penitentiary at Lansing, Kansas, and eight guards were served a late night supper.

Colonel C.S. Pike, who worked within the Harvey system for over fifteen years, was manager of the Harvey House in Arkansas City from 1886 to 1900. Pike, a former newspaperman, was popular with Harvey employees and the community. I believe he is most likely responsible for providing the many insider stories that appeared regularly in the local newspaper during his tenure—tales that the Fred Harvey Company would have never approved of, such as the story reporting that in fourteen hours a Harvey employee caught 203 rats in a trap. One can only hope this took place in a storage building or structure that was not part of the restaurant.

Pike took great pride in the appearance of the Ark City Harvey House and proclaimed it "one of the best on the Harvey system." For the Easter season one year, he had the head cook, Jacob Langousky, color a large number of eggs and arrange them in decorated baskets for table decorations.

In 1926, Alyce LaMotte Barnett's husband died, leaving her with an eight-month-old baby girl. She moved back home to live with her parents but needed to find a job and was pleased when she was hired to work at the Ark City Harvey eating house. While performing her Harvey Girl duties, Alyce met Jim Selan, a Santa Fe Railroad employee. James Alfred Selander had come to America from Omskoldsvik, Sweden, and "Americanized" his last name. Family stories don't tell us how he ended up in Arkansas City, Kansas, but we know Jim worked as a brakeman for many years and then moved up to be a train conductor. The couple was married in 1930 and stayed in Arkansas City.

CHANUTE

The new $40,000 depot and Harvey House opened in Chanute in September 1903, replacing a shabby freight house that had previously served as the depot and Harvey lunch counter. A three-story tower was centered in the two-story building, all constructed of red brick with gray trim and a slate roof. The interior of the depot was light oak with a wash of light green. The Harvey House space was light oak trimmed with rich, dark brown paint. The entire building was heated with steam, plumbed and wired for both gas and electricity. The south end of the large building held the ticket office, baggage room, waiting rooms, a large trunk scale recessed into the floor, a parcel room and the Harvey newsstand.

The entire north end was the Harvey House lunchroom, kitchen and large pantry. The wide lunch counter, topped with brown marble, was surrounded with high-backed stools made of polished oak. Behind the counter was a large island, also with a brown marble top, where desserts and fresh fruit were displayed. Large potted plants decorated the room.

The double-hung windows on the second floor were decorated at top center with light stone keystones. The upstairs space had accommodations for Harvey Girls and the Harvey manager, as well as several Santa Fe division offices. In the center of the building, the third level was an observation tower

Harvey House and Santa Fe Depot, Chanute, Kansas. *Courtesy of Michael McMillan.*

from which the yardmaster observed operations. A decade after the opening of the Harvey House, the building was doubled in size, and a large, elegant Harvey dining room was opened to accommodate the increasing number of passengers traveling through Chanute.

A news story in 1911 provides a good cultural setting to help us understand how remarkable it was for young, single women to be working in remote railroad towns. Four women traveling alone earned the headline "Feminine Quartet Caused Curiosity," followed by a second line: "Mysterious delegation furnished topic of conversation for spectators at depot."

A group of four women had arrived at the Chanute depot aboard the northbound train. "All were large and portly. The one who seemed to be the leader was fleshy, with raven black hair. Two of the others had bright, golden-red hair, while the fourth was a negro." The group was reported to have gone "straight to the Harvey House, where they dined. While in there they were accosted by a reporter, but he was promptly squelched by the leader, who coldly informed him that they did not desire to be interviewed." Following their meal, "they calmly resumed their seats in the Pullman car and paid no attention to a crowd of curious ones who grouped about the depot window."

In October 1912, the *Chanute Daily Tribune* reported that because the average temperature of September was five degrees lower than the previous year, the Harvey House ice consumption was 7,200 pounds less than in 1911. The Chanute Harvey House manager, B.B. Stemmins, who along with all Harvey managers sent regular reports to the Harvey headquarters in Kansas City, was surprised with the drop in ice usage. He set about to find the reason and discovered the cooler September temperatures "explained the situation better than anything else."

Fred Harvey coffee was consistently delicious no matter which Harvey House because in each location the Harvey company tested the local water, and if it didn't meet its standards, quality water was brought in by train. At a time when Kansas was in the midst of a long dry period in 1922, Chanute was not experiencing a shortage of water because the nearby Neosho River provided the town with a ready supply. However, the Santa Fe brought water to the Chanute Harvey House in six-thousand-gallon tanks because of the unpleasant odor of the river water caused by runoff from the oil fields in the county.

As new Harvey Houses opened, it was not uncommon for Mr. Harvey to hire experienced European chefs. The immigrant chefs were generally described as temperamental men whose stormy personalities often clashed with the resolute Harvey Girls. Perhaps a chef's responsibilities were particularly difficult to handle regardless of his country of origin. Approximately six weeks after leaving his job as chef at the Chanute Harvey House, Frank Kennedy was charged with murder in St. Joseph, Missouri, where he worked in a hotel owned by the Swift Packing Company. Newspapers reported that Kennedy "shot and killed one of the waiters at the hotel in a fit of rage." The article further explained that while working in Chanute "he was an excellent chef, but had an unmanageable temper. While working here, he formed a dislike for one of the other employes [*sic*] of the [Harvey] eating house and was only prevented from trying to commit murder by the interference of Manager Gilbert McKee and others, who came to the rescue in time. In an interview, McKee stated that he and the chef were always friendly and he regretted Kennedy's departure because of his ability. Further investigation uncovered the fact that the former Harvey chef had killed two other men but escaped legal punishment on each of the previous occasions by pleading insanity and self-defense.

In addition to working with rough characters who might be capable of murder, there were other hazards in the Chanute (and other) Harvey Houses. Twenty-one-year-old Ethel Sherman traveled approximately seventy-five miles to Chanute from her hometown of Paola, Kansas, to work as a Harvey Girl. Ethel had recently recovered from a badly sprained ankle, an on-the-job injury, when she had another painful accident. As the Harvey Girl carried a tray full of newly baked pies from the kitchen into the pantry, she stumbled into a large bucket of very hot water that had been placed too near the swinging doors by the busboy who was cleaning floors. Ethel's injuries were not serious, but the water was hot enough to scald her lower legs. The Santa Fe doctor examined her, and she was sent home in an ambulance.

Harvey managers kept things operating within the Fred Harvey statutes, supervised all Harvey staff and were at the mercy of the Harvey headquarters, which often moved managers between locations. Soon after his promotion from newsstand cashier to manager in 1905, Gilbert McKee had to appear before a local judge because of a complaint filed by a cook, F.H. Seigal, who had been relieved of his responsibilities at the Harvey House. Seigal accused the manager of abuse and foul language and stated that McKee had generally treated him badly. According to the newspaper account, McKee admitted he had fired the cook and "profanely threatened to throw him out of the Harvey House on his head" and was willing to plead guilty to using profane language to "get rid of the case." The judge assessed the Harvey manager a fine of three dollars and court costs, for a total of five dollars and fifty cents, which McKee promptly paid. He then immediately filed a complaint against Seigal for the same charges. The former cook pleaded not guilty, and a number of witnesses were brought in to testify, including some Harvey House employees. Seigal's guilt was clearly established, and he was fined one dollar plus court costs. The article reported that as the former cook had received his final Harvey House paycheck upon dismissal, he quickly took care of this, which brought the matter to an end.

For all the linen tablecloths, china and crystal settings and well-prepared, delicious food, day-to-day operation of a Harvey House in remote Kansas was far from glamorous. Just before noon one day in the fall of 1904, the Chanute Harvey House was closed by quarantine because cashier S.W. O'Brien was diagnosed with smallpox. About the time the smallpox episode was resolved, a sewer line in the depot basement required the closing of the Harvey House for a week.

O'Brien, whose illness was described as mild, was moved to a boxcar outside the Chanute town limits. The Harvey House was thoroughly fumigated and disinfected and reopened two days later after the entire Harvey staff had been vaccinated and relieved of their responsibilities by a temporary staff. It was thought that the cashier contracted the disease from money he handled or from a train passenger. The *Chanute Daily Tribune* reported that, on the day the Harvey establishment was abruptly closed, "the crowd which tried to get into the eating room for dinner became so clamorous after the train arrived from the north that an officer was stationed there to prevent them from making a determined assault upon the door." O'Brien was kept comfortable in his box car accommodations for eight days, and his mother made frequent trips from Kansas City to "converse with him at a distance of some thirty or forty feet." Another employee, Henry Boyd, who was a porter at the Harvey House, was diagnosed with smallpox almost two weeks after the original case was discovered. He was quarantined at home with his wife and child, and business at the Harvey House was not disrupted.

The Harvey House staff was often called on to work extra hours serving special events for local organizations and families. After an evening at the Hetrick Opera House in Chanute, a club of "unmarrieds" were served a ten-course dinner at the Harvey House that didn't end until after 2:00 a.m. We can only hope that the Harvey Girls who served that affair weren't scheduled to feed the early passenger trains the next morning!

Ruby Helen Haynes was born in 1905 on a farm near Chanute. She and her older sister Beulah both worked at the Harvey House in the 1920s in Chanute, and Ruby also worked at the Bisonte Harvey House in Hutchinson,

Kansas. Family stories relate that although Ruby was less than five feet tall, she was a "human dynamo." Ruby and Beulah, as well as their older sister, loved to dance and are remembered as "some of the prettiest that ever lived in Chanute." The sisters lived for a time on the second floor of the Harvey House but also shared space with other Harvey Girls in a nearby boardinghouse for a time.

The Chanute Harvey House restaurant closed in 1931 along with many Harvey Houses during the Depression years. The last passenger train stopped at the depot in April 1972, and the dignified brick building that once housed the Santa Fe Depot and Harvey House was completely vacated by the Santa Fe in 1983. Almost ten years later, almost $2 million in private donations funded restoration of the building. It is now owned by the City of Chanute and contains the Chanute Public Library and the Martin and Osa Johnson Safari Museum.

FORT SCOTT

The large brick "Frisco" depot at Fort Scott, Kansas, contained a large Fred Harvey newsstand and a lunchroom. The depot was built in 1901, and the Harvey businesses opened shortly thereafter. The *Fort Scott Daily Monitor* reported in April 1904 that "the dormitory for the Harvey Eating house people that has been under construction for the past few weeks is nearing completion." Another news story two years later announced that an exterior electrical sign was added to the front of the "Harvey café" and was attracting attention. "It is a box sign, made of glass and contains an incandescent light. Harvey never does anything by halves and the sign is what was expected." The superintendent of the Harvey Houses on the Frisco line, Ralph Whetham, came to Fort Scott in the summer of 1911 to complete plans for a number of improvements scheduled for the restaurant.

The Fort Scott newsstand was one of nineteen during this time period that bore the Fred Harvey name but were located on the Frisco line rather than the ATSF. The St. Louis–San Francisco Railway (affectionately known as the "Frisco") was a St. Louis–based railroad that operated in nine midwestern and southern states from 1876 to 1980. In Kansas, the Frisco ran in the eastern half of the state.

As with all Harvey Houses, the quality of water at the Fort Scott location was a priority. The city water was deemed unsuitable, and clear, clean water

A Fred Harvey lunchroom and newsstand were located in this Frisco depot at Fort Scott, Kansas. The St. Louis–San Francisco Railway (affectionately known as the "Frisco") was a St. Louis–based railroad that operated in nine midwestern and southern states from 1876 to 1980. *Courtesy of Michael McMillan.*

was transported approximately one hundred miles from Eureka Springs in large crated bottles.

Within a decade of establishing Harvey restaurants and newsstands in depots along the Frisco line, Fred Harvey's son, Ford, who became president of the company after his father's death, secured the contract to sell newspapers, fruit, magazines, books and other merchandise on Frisco passenger trains by outbidding the former contractor, Van Noy News Company. The contract secured privileges on over seven thousand miles of tracks of the Frisco.

It appears that Harvey employees—including Harvey Girls—were transferred between all Harvey locations regardless of which railroad line operated the depot. For example, two Fort Scott waitresses "formerly with the Harvey café" in the Fort Scott Frisco depot were transferred to the Alvarado in Albuquerque, New Mexico, a prominent Harvey hotel on the ATSF line. Fort Scott Harvey manager Fred Kihm was later transferred to the Wellington, Kansas Harvey House on the Santa Fe line. It didn't matter which railroad line a passenger traveled, if there was a Harvey House in the depot, the service and food would be of consistent quality.

Throughout its history, the Fred Harvey Company established and suspended affiliations with various railroad lines—not just the ATSF and the Frisco—making the organization's accomplishments even more impressive. All railroad lines that contracted with Fred Harvey used the Harvey reputation to attract passengers, often referring to "All meals by Fred Harvey." Passenger agents for the Santa Fe touted their line as "the one on which Harvey serves all meals. Remember that," implying they were the only one, which was not entirely true.

Although I didn't find specific details of the Harvey/Frisco business relationship, it appears that by the 1930s, the Fred Harvey Company had abandoned many, if not all, of the Frisco line newsstands and restaurants, handing over (or selling?) those operations to the railway company. This is the same timeframe when many Harvey Houses on the ATSF line were closing. Passenger service ended in Fort Scott in 1960, and the Frisco depot was torn down in 1980.

TOPEKA

In 1876, following Fred Harvey's handshake agreement with the ATSF railroad company, he leased the space on the second floor of the wooden, two-story Topeka depot where the railroad had been operating a lunchroom. This first Harvey House might not have been appealing from the outside, but Fred Harvey set about to make a clear statement of what patrons could expect in his restaurants. He transformed the twenty-seat space with fresh paint, changed the menu and reopened under the name "Topeka Harvey House." Who could have known that, within a few years, Harvey Houses would open along the Santa Fe line across the Southwest to California?

A reporter for the *Leavenworth Times* told of a visit to the Topeka Harvey House just a few days after Harvey's transformation:

> *Yesterday passing through Topeka we saw the familiar face of our old friend Guy Potter, at the Depot Eating House. He looked like a gentleman. He invited us in. We went in and found the neatest, cleanest dining hall in the State, everything bran [sic] new. The crockery, cutlery and silver-ware of the choicest patterns, and the table supplied in the best of style. It was a luxury to set [sic] down to such a table. A man who takes such pains to serve the public ought to be rewarded with a liberal patronage. Guy never does anything by halves. Success to the new enterprise.*

A gong similar to this was used by a Harvey employee outside the Harvey House to help passengers locate the restaurant when they stepped off of the train. This brass gong was used at the Topeka Harvey House. *Courtesy of kansasmemory.org, Kansas State Historical Society.*

A description of some of the early customers in the newly established Topeka Harvey House appears occasionally in magazine articles and academic papers, although the source of the information is not clear: "Among the first patrons of the Topeka lunchroom were seventy-six Plains Indians. On November 4, 1876 the group, led by Spotted Dog, Red Tail and Fast Bear, attracted considerable attention as they dined."

Locals and train passengers took note of the Harvey House, and the business soon was thriving. The local newspaper provided a tongue-in-cheek article indicating that the "onward march" of the ATSF railroad might end in Topeka, as travelers might decline to go farther than Topeka once they had eaten at the new Harvey House. "Traffic backed up and it became necessary for the Santa Fe to open similar houses at other points along its right of way in order that the West might not be settled in just one spot."

In the early 1900s, Topeka was one of the sites chosen by Ford Harvey and the president of the Santa Fe for a new depot and Harvey House built using a regional style of architecture. The two-story red brick building was a simple design with white stone trim above the windows. A covered porch stretched the entire length of the building on the side facing the tracks. In 1909, the Topeka Harvey House temporarily broke from the tradition of using a gong outside to lead train passengers to the restaurant. A news article reported, "The Harvey House employee with the white apron does not step out in front of the eating-house with a brass plate and a drum stick to call the hungry ones to lunch any longer. The brass plate and drum stick have given way to a nice new bell with a mild chiming tone. The bell gives much more satisfaction and is more pleasant to hear." Later reports indicate the Topeka restaurant returned to the traditional gong after it was determined that, while a pleasant sound, the chiming bell didn't attract the attention of train passengers. The Topeka dining room served 110, and there were forty-five seats in the lunchroom.

Santa Fe Depot and Harvey House, Topeka, Kansas. *Courtesy of Michael McMillan.*

The Harvey lunchroom in the 1920s, Topeka, Kansas. *Courtesy of kansasmemory.org, Kansas State Historical Society.*

Katherine Brown began her long career as a Harvey Girl when she was twenty-one years old. This was during the Depression, and Katherine explained, "They were asking people to move to work at some of the other Harvey Houses. I was the youngest, so I had to go." She ended up at the Harvey House in Newton, and as so many Harvey Girls did, she met and married a railroad man. "Being a waitress is hard work," Katherine said. "But I liked it and worked for Fred Harvey thirty years."

From time to time, a discussion surfaces about the attitude of the Fred Harvey Company pertaining to the hiring of minorities. In my research, I have found instances of Hispanic and Native American women being hired to work in a local Harvey House in the kitchen or as maids more often than as Harvey Girl waitresses. I have not discovered records indicating African American women were hired, but that doesn't mean it never happened. The Fred Harvey standards and rules were often ignored or modified to meet the demands of keeping a Harvey House restaurant staffed and operating at capacity. The discovery of the name "Lek Saetia" as a Harvey House manager in Topeka certainly caught my attention. Originally from

Topeka, Kansas Harvey Girls in the early 1950s. *Left to right*: Alice Wall, Velma Pummill, Elizabeth McNabney and Clara Conner. *Photo by Mrs. Brad Conner. Courtesy of Helen Collins.*

Thailand, he was employed by Fred Harvey in the early to mid-1960s. Mr. Saetia is credited for introducing a buffet in the Topeka Harvey restaurant on Fridays and Saturdays.

The Santa Fe Depot, freight depot and Santa Fe office building are still standing in Topeka.

WICHITA

The first train to roll through Wichita, Kansas, did so on May 16, 1872. Shortly after the turn of the twentieth century, Wichita was in need of a railroad station that could serve four passenger rail lines at once: the Atchison, Topeka and Santa Fe; Chicago Rock Island; Pacific (Rock Island); St. Louis and San Francisco (Frisco). The stately Union Station was designed by Louis Curtiss. Natural light from large, arched windows illuminated the marble walls and ceilings and tile floors. Within the fifty-seven-thousand-

Harvey Girls served train passengers in the large Fred Harvey lunchroom in Union Station in Wichita, Kansas. *Courtesy of Michael McMillan.*

square-foot building was a Fred Harvey Lunch Room with a semicircular marble lunch counter surrounded by seventy-seven stools. Marble-topped serving tables displayed fresh fruit and desserts. Bustling Union Station greeted many travelers and was a place to get a haircut, get shoes shined or enjoy a quick lunch. Tunnels ran under the tracks, supplying the cavernous building with steam heat.

In 1914, the *Wichita Beacon* announced, "The Harvey Girl Comes to Wichita." The news story noted that Harvey Girls had become synonymous with the transportation industry:

> *You'll recognize her. Suppose you have arisen from a sleeper with your ears filled with cinders and a grouch so black you can taste it. You disgustedly enter the lunch room with your feelings written on your face. Your greatest wish then is to break up the furniture and china. From a large door in sails the girl in question, all smiles and like a spring sunrise.*
>
> *"What would you wish this morning? Strawberries and cream, cakes or ham and—" you know how the lingo goes and how hard you fall for it. Your crustiness disappears in the steam from the flaky cakes and the cream on the strawberries is as sweet as your disposition. She did this in the famous Fred Harvey method of pleasing. She was a typical Harvey girl.*

Eight of them trot miles in their circular track in the station lunch room every day. They seldom try sprinkling one with hot bouillon and a switched order is unusual. Harvey girls after all are more than waitresses. They are part of a great system to provide comfort for the man, woman or child who travels. You get a smile with a ten cent sandwich which is just as cheery as the one given the fat man who ordered a dollar dinner.

The famous Fred Harvey discovered that this new smile seasoning made everything taste better and maybe that's the reason the Union Station room is popular.

The convergence of four rail lines in the early 1900s brought celebrities through Union Station, and the Harvey Girls were there twenty-four hours a day, seven days a week to serve whoever sat down at the lunch counter. On tour of the United States, famous Scottish soprano Mary Garden stopped in the Harvey House and ordered coffee and apple pie at 1:00 a.m. The waitress who took her order described the well-dressed performer sitting at the counter: "Dangling her feet on the brass counter rail like a drummer [traveling salesman]. The Harvey chef warmed the pie, gave it a pinch of extra spice and sent it in with a smile." Harvey employees were taught to treat all customers the same, extending the same efficient service to each person. They were also trained to exchange in conversation only what was necessary to provide that service. No informal small talk was allowed.

The Wichita Harvey House lunchroom closed in 1935. The last passenger train to stop at Union Station in Wichita, Kansas, was the Amtrak Lone Star #16. When it left on October 6, 1979, Union Station's passenger depot days were over.

Current photos of the interior of the Union Station building show the preserved, original Fred Harvey Lunch Room sign at the entrance to the space where the restaurant served train passengers and local residents.

After purchasing the century-old Union Station in downtown Wichita two years ago, Occidental Management has begun a $54 million renovation and expansion on the historic real estate.

6

HARVEY SERVICE ON THE GO

Newsstands and Carts

As the Santa Fe and Fred Harvey were raising the standard of service to train passengers, it became obvious that the magazines, candy, cigars and other merchandise sold by railway news concessions were greatly missing the mark. Once again, the Harvey company proved its capabilities.

In a sense, Fred Harvey Newsstands were the twentieth-century forerunner of modern-day convenience stores, and every Harvey House had a newsstand. In some Harvey House locations, the newsstand was inside the Harvey Lunch Room; however, in larger train depots, it was usually a separate shop that opened into the waiting room and onto the platform beside the train tracks. The amount and variety of merchandise offered was in proportion to the number of passengers passing through the train station.

In Kansas, at the following depots, the only Fred Harvey business was newsstands or sandwich carts: Lawrence, Leavenworth, Ottawa and Pittsburg.

The only Harvey presence in Lawrence may have been the newsstand in the depot; however, in the early 1920s, young Lawrence girls were provided the opportunity to learn the Harvey Girl ways. Seven young women were given the opportunity to earn part of their next semester's university expenses by traveling to Las Vegas, New Mexico, and Barstow, California, to work in Harvey Houses there.

The students received standard Harvey Girl benefits—free train pass, room, board and laundry service—although their monthly pay of twenty dollars was about half what full-time Harvey waitresses were being paid. The summer waitresses were required to serve lunch at the lunch counter

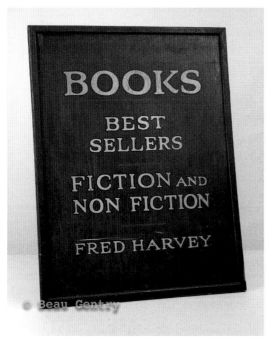

Left: A Harvey newsstand sign used to encourage customers to stop and consider the latest books for sale. Beginning in the early 1900s, the Fred Harvey Company became a significant influence on what books became bestsellers simply by promoting them at its newsstands. Well into the 1940s, book publishers would use Harvey newsstand sales to dictate print orders. *Photo by Beau Gentry. Courtesy of Skip Gentry's Fred Harvey Memorabilia Collection.*

Below: The Santa Fe Depot, Lawrence, Kansas. The Fred Harvey Company had a large newsstand in this depot. *Courtesy of Michael McMillan.*

but were given an abundance of free time to explore the area. The Kansas girls were the first to participate in the summer program created by the Harvey company; however, I was unable to document whether the program continued beyond that initial summer.

The Fred Harvey family home, Leavenworth, Kansas. The house is on the National Register of Historic Places in the United States and is being transformed into the National Fred Harvey Museum. *Wikimedia Commons/Public Domain.*

Although the Harvey family made their home in Leavenworth and that is where Fred Harvey died, the city's ranking as a railroad center warranted only a Harvey newsstand. Mr. Harvey and his wife, Sally, along with their five children—Ford, Minnie, Marie, Byron and Sybil—settled in Leavenworth and in 1883 purchased a two-story stone house situated at Seventh and Olive Streets. The impressive structure was built of cream-colored Junction City limestone and sat on an acre. The Leavenworth Historical Museum

Association now owns the Harvey family house and is in the process of renovating the building and then converting it into a Fred Harvey museum.

Ottawa began as the division headquarters of the Southern Kansas Railway Company from Ottawa to Chanute. In the late 1880s, the headquarters were moved to Chanute. In 1920, there were newspaper stories announcing the possibility of a Harvey House "near the Santa Fe station in Ottawa." At this time, there were two sets of plans in the architect's office in Topeka, Kansas. One set was for a new hotel and restaurant to be built adjacent to the depot. The other was for construction of only a restaurant next to the depot.

Unfortunately, neither plan developed into reality, and there was never a Harvey House in Ottawa. However, passengers and railroad employees were provided limited access to good food from a Fred Harvey sandwich cart in the Santa Fe Depot. Although there isn't much information available about the Harvey sandwich carts, most certainly they were used throughout the system in depot locations that did not merit a Harvey lunch counter.

One of nineteen Harvey newsstands operating on the Frisco Line was in Pittsburg, Kansas. This newsstand had a prominent place within the Frisco depot where customers could view merchandise and make purchases from inside or trackside through a large window.

Cigarettes and cigars were the prominent merchandise in every Fred Harvey Newsstand. Large Lucky Strike posters featuring young beauties in shorts and ballet slippers declared, "It's toasted!" and "Lucky's are always kind to your throat!" Colorful advertising touted such products as "flat fifties," cigarette tins popular in the 1940s. The American Tobacco Company included this message inside the tins: "These LUCKY STRIKE CIGARETTES will commend themselves to your critical approval. The additional 'toasting process' adds to the character and improves the taste of the fine tobacco." The Fred Harvey private brand of cigars, as well as Roi-Tan, Cremo and Prodigo, was sold with the promise: "We give discount on cigars bought by the box."

Chewing gum and candy were big sellers, and the newsstands were always framed with wire displays of postcards. The postcard business flourished after 1904, when Ford Harvey began working with the Detroit Publishing Company, which had developed a process for colorizing black-and-white photos. A good number of the postcards from the early Harvey days have survived and are often offered online. Many of the images in this book were digitized from original Harvey postcards from the private collection of Michael McMillan.

Souvenirs were attractively displayed to appeal to train passengers. Keychains and letter openers, as well as figurines and toy trucks, all clamored for the traveler's attention. Displayed on glass shelves, small items were advertised as souvenirs for bridge prizes. The variety of merchandise was endless: Cloisonné compacts, sewing notions, watches and brightly colored felt triangular pennants emblazoned with the state's name: "KANSAS."

At the age of twelve, Ed John was a self-described "knee-panted" boy who worked after school and on Saturdays and Sundays delivering the *Emporia Gazette*. "During the time I delivered papers, each day we were given two extra copies of the paper to cover any miss-throws on our route. There was a pair of eastbound trains that departed Emporia between 5:00 p.m. and 6:00 p.m. If I was lucky I could get back to the depot in time to sell the extra papers in the men's waiting room. I had to hustle, but that would make me an extra dime for my evening's work, and in the winter I could be inside for a while and get warm." One evening, a special officer (railroad policeman) stopped the young man and told him he couldn't sell papers on railroad property. "He told me that Fred Harvey had the paper selling rights so that ended that little caper for me."

"Things have a way of working out if you are patient," Ed said. "Wilford Vestal, Harvey newsstand manager, broke his hip, and when it healed he

Harvey agents used cases such as this to carry the latest newspapers and magazines to sell to train passengers. In remote areas, folks depended on Fred Harvey for the latest news. *Photo by Beau Gentry. Courtesy of Skip Gentry's Fred Harvey Memorabilia Collection.*

The news service was an important part of Fred Harvey's service to train passengers and another example of how closely Harvey worked with the Santa Fe Railroad. Newspapers and perhaps small items to sell such as postcards were transported in trunks and sold to passengers on the train. *Photo by Beau Gentry. Courtesy of Skip Gentry's Fred Harvey Memorabilia Collection.*

couldn't walk very well and he needed someone to help him open up in the morning. I got the job of picking up the out-of-town newspapers at the express office and the baggage room before I went to school. I also stocked the fresh fruit sold at the newsstand." Ed doesn't remember getting any money for this job; instead, he would get an empty orange or apple box. "This wasn't too bad because the side boards of the box were just the ticket for my coping saw, and the box ends made swell kindling wood. I tended two fires at home." Soon, the young man was given the opportunity to sell papers on a 20 percent commission basis. "No sales, no pay," Ed explained. "But sometimes you might see a movie star on the California Limited or maybe a woman smoking a cigarette! Thus I became a Fred Harvey employee." At this time, the newsstand manager had a staff of four boys under the age of fifteen: two ice cream boys, a fruit boy and a paperboy. The boys were paid weekly in cash.

Within a year, Ed was given the summer job of selling ice cream outside the Emporia Harvey House. "This was the best platform job of all because a guy could make, maybe, two dollars a day." Ed would place a wire order every evening to Newton, Kansas, where the ice cream was made in the

Harvey creamery. The ice cream arrived in Emporia at noon the next day. Ed was still earning a 20 percent commission, only now for ice cream cones instead of newspapers. "On a normal day, I could move three gallons of ice cream a day. On a really good day, I could double that. I didn't go to work until almost noon when the Chief would be rolling into Emporia. The last train of the day would arrive around 6:10 p.m. So I loafed between trains and could read all the magazines from the newsstand that I wished, and for free." Ed wore an all-white uniform with a black tie and dispensed the hand-cranked ice cream from a small refrigerated cart. "My friends were working hard trying to find lawns to mow. Not me—I'd rather sell an ice cream cone." Ed Johnson worked at the Emporia Harvey newsstand for almost ten years. Many years later, Ed commented that he had a lot of fun working for Fred Harvey. "The newsstand managers taught me many basic principles of business and the art of serving the public."

Luella Chambers Hunsaker began work at the Newton Harvey Newsstand in 1945, when she was fifteen. "I got the job at that young age because my brother worked for the husband of the newsstand manager," Luella explained. "I worked there all through high school." She was the cashier and clerk and worked full-time during the summer. The newsstand opened into the restaurant area near the double counters in the lunchroom. "During the school year I worked Sunday through Thursday and on Saturday. I was off on Friday so I could attend school activities." As was typical at Harvey newsstands, Luella sold magazines, postage stamps and, in addition to all Kansas newspapers, the *Chicago Tribune*. "We also had gift items for sale. Things like boxes of soap, little metal Scottie dogs on a magnetic base and a pair of Indian dolls in suede costumes."

Young women who worked in the newsstands were required to wear a different uniform than Harvey Girls, and men wore suits. "My uniform was very uncomfortable. It was a very heavy tan material, trimmed in dark brown. There was a Fred Harvey shield on one of the sleeves," Luella said. "That was one of the most fun jobs I ever had. One day Bob Hope walked in! There was a fellow walking a few feet behind him that we all thought was probably his bodyguard. Mr. Hope bought a movie magazine and gave me his autograph." She recalled a time when Duke Ellington and his band had a layover in Newton: "Mr. Ellington walked out on the platform in his smoking jacket." Luella also met Eddie Cantor, a popular singer of the time. "His hit song was 'Ida,' and that was the name of one of the Harvey Girls. He sang the song to her in the lunchroom." After finishing high school, Luella moved to California, and

Luella Chambers considered her job as cashier and clerk in the Newton Harvey Newsstand the "most fun job" she ever had. *Courtesy of Luella Chambers Hunsaker.*

a few years after marrying, she, her husband and their two sons moved back to Kansas.

In 1939, after many Harvey Houses had closed, an article in the *Chicago American* provided a glimpse into the still extensive Fred Harvey newsstand system:

Underneath the station [Chicago Union Station] level with the Chicago River, is the heart of the Fred Harvey system. A maze of storerooms and kitchens forms a network of many miles. More than 60,000 different articles are kept there. William R. Ryan, in charge of the cigar, paper and magazine counters, said: "We sell everything from pins to needles, blankets, cigars, imported perfumes…in fact, the only thing that we don't sell are farm implements. Our organization educated department stores to the fact that toys can be sold the entire year, not just at Christmas time. We make our own shirts, hats and ties for the Fred Harvey men's shops."

Ryan further explained that Fred Harvey sausage was made in Kansas City and shipped to Chicago to store in refrigerators underneath Union Station. Items stored in this extensive underground pantry were sold in Chicago; however, they were also shipped to the Harvey newsstands still serving train passengers.

Fred Harvey newsstands were a very successful business, and throughout the Harvey system, many survived long after lunchrooms and dining rooms had closed. Fred Harvey business records indicated that by 1950, the company still maintained over one hundred newsstands.

7

FROM THE KITCHEN

Harvey House Recipes

Harvey House recipes were featured in the *Santa Fe Employes'* [*sic*] magazine in the "Harvey Service" column. These recipes are reproduced here just as they were used in Harvey kitchens. Each time I read these recipes, I try to imagine the Harvey House kitchen staff putting together a meal for hungry train passengers with approximately thirty minutes to eat. Certainly, some things were prepared in advance, but a strict Fred Harvey rule was that the food would be fresh. I suppose the chef knew measurements from experience, and he passed this information on to the staff. A common Harvey Girl story relates the difficulty of dealing with the grumpy chef. In defense of the chef, consider using the vague instructions of these recipes and cooking for forty-plus diners on a stove fueled with coal. I would be grumpy, too. In later years, Harvey recipes were printed on a standard form and distributed to each Harvey House kitchen.

Chocolate Puffs

Boil together a cup of flour, a cup of water, and half a cup of butter. Remove from the fire, beat in an ounce of melted chocolate and (one at a time) three eggs. Bake in a gem pan, then cut off the top of each cake and put in a teaspoon of strawberry preserves. Cover with sweetened whipped cream.

Dandelion Salad

Wash, pick over, and cook dandelions until tender in boiling water to which has been added one-eighth teaspoonful soda. Add together one Neufchatel cheese, four hard boiled eggs, three-quarters of a cup of cooked dandelions, olive oil, one-quarter teaspoon of salt, one-eighth teaspoon of cayenne. Rub through a strainer, add the egg yolks and the dandelions separately; add oil until of a consistency to handle; salt and cayenne. Mix thoroughly and, when well blended, shape into balls. Serve on white leaves of lettuce, with French mayonnaise or boiled dressing.

Tomato and Green Pepper Salad

Cut rather thick slices of peeled tomatoes and spread each with finely chopped green pepper, mixed with French dressing; on each one put three very tiny white onions, cooked and peeled, with French dressing over all.

French Dressing

Taragon vinegar, one part; olive oil, four parts; paprika, salt and pepper. Mix very thoroughly, having a piece of ice in the bowl.

[Note: although Fred Harvey would not sanction the use of anything but olive oil of the very highest grade, those to whom the flavor of olive oil is distasteful will find peanut oil an excellent substitute. It is much less expensive and cuts the vinegar equally as well, producing a most palatable dressing.]

Fried Green Tomatoes

Cut into thin slices some large, perfectly green specimens (they must not have begun to show any sign of ripening, and those freshly pulled are really best for this dish). Sprinkle with salt and dip in cornmeal until covered. Fry in a little butter until a nice brown. Cover the frying pan throughout the cooking process to keep the tomatoes tender. Serve either plain or with a brown sauce.

Bell Pepper (Fred Harvey Style)

Six skinned bell peppers (enough to make twelve orders); two to three onions; three ounces of butter or olive oil; one green pepper; a tablespoon of flour; one crushed clove of garlic; three or four egg plants; two whole eggs; one half-pint of milk; a handful of fresh bread crumbs. Remove the skin from the peppers by dipping them into hot grease. Peel the egg plant and dice a quarter of an inch thick. Cut the peppers in two lengthwise, remove the fleshy part adhering to the seeds, chop it and add to the egg plant. Cut the onions and green peppers fine; put on the fire with oil or butter and let cook for ten minutes. Add the crumbs, garlic, egg plant, a little salt and stir frequently until done. Add the flour; mix well; pour in the milk; let come to a boil and keep stirring. Add the eggs and a little chopped parsley. Mix well, season if necessary and remove from the fire. Stuff the bell peppers with this mixture. Sprinkle with grated cheese; put a small lump of butter on each one and leave them in a hot oven long enough to produce a nice golden brown.

Chicken à la King

Take the breasts of tender fowls, slice in size desired. Let simmer in fresh butter a while. Add for one fowl two gills (one-half pint) of sherry wine; one small cupful of cream. Season to taste. Beat together four yolks of eggs and a quarter cupful of cream. Parboil and dice one green pepper, one sweet pepper; slice four mushrooms. Mix all ingredients together.

Mackerel Baked in Cream

Skin, bone and divide a large fish into four pieces, season and fry in butter, drain it and put the pan where it will keep hot. Mix half a pint of white stock, or Bechamel sauce, with the yolk of an egg, stir over the fire for a minute or two, pour over the fish and put chopped parsley and onions and breadcrumbs over the top of the fish.

Lamb Chops à la Nelson

Make a dressing of boiled onions and grated cheese, passing through a sieve; broil chop on one side only, cover the unbroiled side with dressing and place in hot oven to brown; garnish with tongue tips and mushroom tops.

German Potato Salad

Boil twelve potatoes. While hot cut in thin slices, cover with finely sliced onions and add one teaspoonful of salt and one half-teaspoonful of pepper. Mix the yolk of one egg with three tablespoonsful of olive oil and four tablespoonsful of vinegar. Pour the well-mixed dressing over the potatoes, then pour a half-cupful of boiling water or broth over the whole mixture and stir well. Sprinkle with chopped parsley; cover and let stand for a few hours. This salad never will be dry.

Cocoanut Bars

Five whites of eggs beaten very stiff; add ten ounces of granulated sugar, seven ounces of cocoanut; mix together, spread on wafer paper and cut in finger shapes. Place on buttered pans and bake in a cool oven.

Rice Pudding

Wash and boil two tablespoonsful of rice in water to cover. Dissolve a quarter of a boxful of gelatin in cold water and stir into the rice while hot. Allow this to cool, then add a cupful of sugar, two tablespoonsful of chopped, preserved figs. Put on ice several hours. Serve with whipped cream.

Banana Pie

Peel and slice the bananas thin, add sugar, a little butter and some spice, allspice or a dash of ginger, a little acid syrup, lemon or orange juice. Bake with full cover or put on a meringue when done. Another way is to make a syrup with one-half pint of water and vinegar, one pound of sugar and some allspice, and season the bananas with the syrup.

Cranberry Sherbet

Place one quart of cranberries in three cups of boiling water and let boil about ten minutes. When the berries are well softened, strain through a sieve. Let one and one-half cupsful of sugar, in one quart of water, boil twenty minutes. Add one tablespoonful of gelatin that has been soaked in two tablespoons of cold water. When cool, strain and add the cranberries, with more sugar if desired. Then freeze as usual.

French Apple Pie with Nutmeg Sauce

Eight cups sliced, tart apples; one-half cup water; one and one-half cups sugar; one recipe plain pastry: one cup all-purpose flour; one-half cup sugar; one-third cup butter; one cup graham crackers crushed; few drops of vanilla. For sauce mix one egg yolk; one-half cup sugar; one cup milk. Heat to the boiling point; remove from heat and add nutmeg. Cook apples in water until tender; add sugar and mix carefully to retain shape of apples. Arrange apples in pastry lined pie plate. Combine graham cracker crumbs, flour, sugar, butter and vanilla. Mix until it resembles coarse crumbs, sprinkle mixture over apples. Bake in hot oven ten minutes, then in moderate oven twenty minutes.
Serve with Nutmeg Sauce.

Beef Rissoles

Cold cooked beef, minced, three parts, and grated bread crumbs, one part; mix and season with herbs, grated rind of lemon, salt and pepper, bound with raw yolks of eggs, made into the shape of an egg, breaded and fried. Serve with a mound of mashed potatoes in the center of the dish, a rissole at each end and side, with some thickened roast beef gravy poured around. Garnish potatoes with parsley. This dish may also be served with kidney beans, green peas, French string beans or mixed vegetables instead of the potatoes.

Meat Pie, Potato Crust

Cut cold roast beef in thin slices, removing all fat and gristle. Cover the bones and trimmings with cold water; add a few slices of onions and carrots, also a stalk of celery. Let simmer two hours. Strain off the broth and simmer in it the slices of beef until they are tender. Season with salt and pepper and sprinkle with flour. Cover with a potato crust, leaving an opening at the top. Bake for fifteen minutes.

Swedish Meat Balls

One pound of lean pork shoulder; eight small toasts; three boiled potatoes; one onion. Put all ingredients through a grinder, emptying into a bowl. Then add two eggs, and salt and pepper to taste. Work together thoroughly and make them into balls, then fry.

Clam Soup

One heaping tablespoon of butter and two of flour, rubbed into a cream. Melt in a saucepan over the fire and add slowly a quart of rich milk, stirring constantly; when it thickens add celery salt, a bit of cayenne and a cup of minced clams with their juice; let it come to a boil and serve.

Macaroni and Oysters

Cook macaroni in salted water, without breaking it, till it is soft. Butter a covered mold or small pail quite thickly, and, beginning in the center of the bottom, coil the macaroni around. As it begins to rise on the sides put in a layer of oysters, only half cooked, mixed with a thick cream sauce, and then add more macaroni, and so on until the mold is full. Put on the cover and cook in a kettle of boiling water for half an hour. Turn out on a hot platter and surround with cheese balls made by adding melted butter and chopped parsley to grated American cheese and molding into shape. Pass a bowl of cream sauce with this.

Scrapple

One pound of sausage meat; one tablespoon of salt; four quarts of cold water; one pound of cornmeal. The sausage should be mixed first with a small quantity of water until the particles are separated, then the mixture should be boiled hard before adding the meal, very slowly at first, stirring continually with a wooden spoon or ladle. Add the meal as in making mush, never allowing it to stop boiling, and when it is the consistency of a stiff batter, turn it into moistened pans until the next morning. It should be sliced and then fried crisp in hot fat and served.

Eggs en Fromage

Beat six eggs very slightly. Place in a chafing dish a tablespoon of butter, and when this is hot throw into it two heaping tablespoons of finely grated hard cheese. Stir about until smoothly creamed in the butter, then add the eggs, season with paprika and a little salt, and cook until the eggs are slightly scrambled. Serve on toast.

Escalloped Egg Plant

Peel two large egg plants; boil until very tender; drain, chop fine, and season to taste with butter, salt and pepper, put into an earthen pudding dish and cover the top with an inch layer of bread crumbs sprinkled with salt and dotted with bits of butter. Bake in a moderate oven until it is a rich brown.

Stuffed Onions

Parboil in salt water for twenty minutes some large white onions; drain and let cool. Take out the inner parts of the onions with a tablespoon or large vegetable scoop. Add to these two handfuls of bread crumbs and two of mushrooms. Chop the whole fine, put it in a saucepan with a ladleful of drawn butter and tomatoes chopped fine, parsley, salt and pepper. Mix well. Stuff the onions, then put them in a flat saucepan and sprinkle with bread crumbs and a little butter. Bake for about half an hour until a light brown color.

English Plum Pudding

One pound of suet, chopped fine; two dozen crackers, rolled fine; one pound of raisins; one pound of currants; six eggs; one nutmeg; one cup of sugar; a little salt. Sift a little flour over the mixture—just enough to keep it together. Tie in a cloth, allowing space in which to swell, and boil constantly about five hours. Then turn out onto a platter. Serve hot or cold. Use any preferred sauce.

Chestnut Pudding

Peel and boil three pints of chestnuts until tender, remove the skins and press through a sieve. Mix with one-half pound of butter, three-quarters of a pound of sugar, two cups of sweet milk and four well-beaten eggs. Flavor with vanilla. Beat well together, pour into a buttered pudding mold, cover tightly and steam for one hour. Serve very hot with orange syrup and sections of candied orange.

BIBLIOGRAPHY

Anschutz, Philip F. *Out Where the West Begins: Profiles, Visions & Strategies of Early Western Business Leaders*. Denver, CO: Cloud Camp Press, LLC, 2015.

Bell, James B. *Ghost Trains: Images from America's Railroad Heritage*. New York: Chartwell Books, 2014.

City of Coolidge. *History of Coolidge, (Kansas) 1886–1986*. Holly, CO: Holly Publishing Co., 1986.

Dugan, Brenna Stewart. "Girls Wanted: For Service at the Fred Harvey Houses." Graduate thesis, Texas Tech University, December 2008.

Foster, George H., and Peter C. Weiglin. *The Harvey House Cookbook*. Atlanta, GA: Longstreet Press, 1992.

Fried, Stephen. *Appetite for America: Fred Harvey and the Business of Civilizing the Wild West—One Meal at a Time*. New York: Random House, 2010.

Grattan, Virginia L. *Mary Colter: Builder upon the Red Earth*. Flagstaff, AZ: Northland Press, 1980.

Henderson, James D. *Meals by Fred Harvey: A Phenomenon of the American West*. Fort Worth: Texas Christian University Press, 1969.

Kaufmann, Gina. *More Than Petticoats: Remarkable Kansas Women*. Guilford, CT: Morris Book Publishing, LLC, 2012.

Latimer, Rosa Walston. *Harvey Houses of New Mexico: Historic Hospitality from Raton to Deming*. Charleston, SC: The History Press, 2015.

———. *Harvey Houses of Texas: Historic Hospitality from the Gulf Coast to the Panhandle*. Charleston, SC: The History Press, 2014.

Marshall, James. *Santa Fe: The Railroad That Built an Empire*. New York: Random House, 1945.

Poling-Kempes, Lesley. *The Harvey Girls: Women Who Opened the West*. New York: Paragon House, 1989.

Sandy, Wilda, and Larry K. Hancks. *Stalking Louis Curtiss*. Kansas City, MO: Ward Parkway Press, 1991.

INDEX

ABOUT THE AUTHOR

Rosa Walston Latimer owns an independent bookstore and is a playwright and an award-winning photographer. She has written for national and regional magazines and newspapers and was news editor of a print and an online newspaper and supervising director of a nationally syndicated television program.

The story of her Harvey Girl grandmother sparked her interest in preserving women's history. After being told by a museum curator in another state that there were no Harvey Houses in Texas,  she was determined to preserve this important part of the state's railroad history and inspired to write her first book, *Harvey Houses of Texas: Historic Hospitality from the Gulf Coast to the Panhandle*. Latimer has now chronicled her grandmother's story, as well as the stories of many other New Mexico Harvey Girls, in her second book, *Harvey Houses of New Mexico: Historic Hospitality from Raton to Deming*. While working on these books, she realized the Kansas Harvey story should be told—after all, Kansas is where the Harvey House story began. Latimer's third book in the Harvey House series is *Harvey Houses of Kansas: Historic Hospitality from Topeka to Syracuse*.

The author lives above her bookstore in a two-story, historic building. She shares the upstairs space with her three rescue dogs. Downstairs, the bookstore cat, Ruby, happily greets customers and watches the traffic on Main Street. Rosa is actively involved in the arts and historical preservation of her community, and gallery space in her bookstore features regional artists. She is currently working on a book about three significant historic hotels in Las Vegas, New Mexico, and has begun research for a fourth book in the Harvey House series.